MW00439132

Yellowstone & Grand Teton

A Comprehensive Guide to Outdoor Activities

Matt Harding & Freddie Snalam

UNIQUE ADVENTURE GUIDES

All drawings, unless otherwise credited, by Freddie Snalam.
All photographs, unless otherwise credited, are by the authors.

*Cover photograph: Hiking the Garnet Canyon Trail in
Grand Teton National Park*

All rights reserved. No part of this book may be reproduced or transmitted in any form or by any means, electronic or mechanical, including photocopying, recording or by any information storage and retrieval system without written permission from the publisher, except for the inclusion of brief quotations in a review.

First Edition
Copyright ©1995 All Points Publishing, Inc.
PO Box 4832, Boulder, CO. 80306 USA.

ISBN 1-884294-01-4

Printed in the United States of America
10 9 8 7 6 5 4 3 2 1

Published by:
All Points Publishing, Inc.
PO Box 4832,
Boulder,
Colorado, 80306,
USA.

C O N T E N T S

WARNING - DISCLAIMER

This book is designed to provide information with regard to sporting activities. It is highly likely that, despite our best efforts, mistakes have crept in. The authors do not suggest that anyone in particular participate in any of the sports described herein. It is impossible for us to guess anyone's skill or judgement and suitability for any of these activities.

Be aware that many of these activities are potentially strenuous with inherent risks and dangers. Hazards, whether natural or manmade, whether included in the text or not, can present themselves at any time. It is the reader's responsibility to ensure that they have sufficient skill and fitness to participate in the activities.

The purpose of this book is to educate and entertain. The authors and the publisher shall have neither liability nor responsibility to any person or entity with respect to any injury, loss or damage caused, or alleged to be caused, directly or indirectly, by the information contained in this book.

Ride 'Em Cowboy - Jackson Town Square.

Notes on using this guide

Distances: Distances given for trails are for an out-and-back trip, and are approximate.

Difficulty: Judging relative difficulty of trails is by its nature, an inexact science. We have worked on the assumption that an Easy trail can be completed by a person of average fitness, with little or no experience, in the time allocated. A Moderate rated trail will be longer, more difficult, and will require more effort. A Difficult trail will always include technical difficulty, some risk, and will almost always be long and arduous.

We recommend that before setting out on a Difficult trail, you assess one of the easier trails in the book to see how it fits with your own level of competency.

Time Required: As with judging difficulty, giving a probable time required is never straightforward. We have erred on the safe side, and as a result, you may well find that you can do the trail in a faster time. We do feel it is important, particularly when in the mountains, to allow plenty of time in case of route finding problems, other hazards, or even to take in the sights without having to rush.

Start Elevation & Elevation Gain: Again these are approximate, and are intended to give some idea of the amount of height gain on a trail. They only take in the lowest point and the highest, and do not include cumulative height gain.

Best Time Of Year: This purely gives an idea as to when the trail will be at its best. It cannot, however, take into account weather variations, year to year. For instance, some mountain passes will be clear of snow earlier in the season some years than in others. The only reliable, current, source of information is the Park Rangers, and we recommend always talking to them before setting out on long trails.

National Parks & Forests: As this guide covers an area that includes National Parks, National Forest, Wilderness Areas and private land, it is important to note that different regulations covering activities within these areas exist. We have tried to make sure that the text includes these regulations where appropriate, but as these are subject to change, you are strongly advised when entering a Park to enquire at the Entrance Station, or at a Visitor Center, as to the current situation regarding the activity you wish to undertake. This is not only useful for checking regulations, it is also a good idea as the Park Rangers have a wide experience of the area, and can offer advice as well.

Maps: The maps we have included in the book are strictly intended as a guide to understanding where the route goes, the terrain and the sights along the way. They are not to scale, and features may not be exactly placed. They are not designed to be used for navigational purposes. All visitors to the area who wish to explore the backcountry are strongly advised to get a map for this purpose. Trails Illustrated produce a map of each Park, as does Earthwalk Press. These maps are widely available in Visitors Centers throughout the Parks.

A key to the maps is on page 15.

INTRODUCTION

The Greater Yellowstone Region offers a surprisingly diverse range of activities within some of the most awe-inspiring country found anywhere in the world. From the dramatic peaks of the Tetons to the startling colors of the Grand Canyon of the Yellowstone to the grandeur of the wildlife, ample rewards await the traveler.

When Yellowstone National Park was originally established in 1872, few could have foreseen the effect such an act would have on recreation in the following century world-wide. From this seed grew the process by which large areas of land throughout the world have been set aside both as a resource for recreation, and perhaps more importantly, as a way of preserving some of the finest lands.

Yellowstone National Park now receives almost 4 million visitors a year, most of whom seem to be visiting at the same time as you. And in some ways it is starting to show. It can be almost stiflingly crowded in places, and the wilderness lover may wonder whether they should have stayed at home. Despair not! It only takes a few minutes to get away from the crowds. All it takes is a bit of energy to walk or cycle away from the roads and solitude may be yours. True, some of the best-known trails can be busy at peak times, particularly in Grand Teton National Park, but even there, a walk of a mile or two will put most people behind you. Also, in a typical year, approximately 70% of the visitors visit the region during July and August. Plan accordingly!

The purpose of this guide is to help you find ways to enjoy your visit, be it long or short, with the emphasis on *outdoor activities*. Most of the activities in this book will require effort, perhaps even some risk, but the rewards, we think, far outweigh the hazards. Things of value are rarely easily attained, and for some, the battle is part of the value.

Geology

Grand Teton National Park

The youngsters of the Rocky Mountains Range, this group of mountains were formed a mere 9 million years ago. The cause of their formation was a break in the earth's crust along a 40 mile crack known as the Teton Fault. The western section, or block, lifted skyward to form the Tetons. The eastern block slipped downward to form the area now known as Jackson Hole. The lower block fell a distance 4 times greater than the rise of the upper block.

Since then, wind, glacial ice and water immediately began eroding the land to form the skyline that we see today. Displacement or building of rocks continue to this day and earthquakes (albeit small) could still occur along this fault.

Today many of the valleys have the U-shaped appearance caused by the movements of ice during the ice age. Prior to this, the valleys were cut by water, and as a result were V shaped. Glacial action moved vast quantities of rock, sometimes great distances. Natural dams were formed, leading to the creation of lakes that still exist today, such as Jenny, Leigh, Bradley and Taggart Lakes. Jackson Lake was formed by melt water from the snowcap that covered part of Yellowstone.

Yellowstone National Park

Two opposite elements, namely fire and ice, are amongst the main ingredients for the formation of what is now know as Yellowstone.

About 60 million years ago, all hell broke loose when volcanoes here spewed forth a mixture of gas and rock particles and fragments. For millions of years after, countless eruptions followed, spreading layers if lava over the region. About 40 million years ago, this came to an end, and the area entered a relatively quiet period. Some 2½ million years ago the Ice Age came to this region, and thanks to glaciation, what had been a ongoing erosion process was speeded up dramatically. The great North American Ice Cap that covered much of the USA did not reach Yellowstone. Instead its own glaciers were formed in the high plateaus. These went to work substantially changing the landscape from about 300,000 years ago to the most recent period about 8,500 years ago.

Meanwhile, about 2 million years ago there was the first of three huge volcanic eruptions, the others being at 1,200,000 and 600,000 years ago, in the area. The Central Region of what is now the park subsequently collapsed forming a deep depression, also know as a caldera. The force behind this, magma, still powers the geysers and hot springs in the Park. Yellowstone has about 200 geysers, which actually form more than half the geysers in the world. There are also thousands of other thermal features in the Park, forming the last great thermal region in the world that is still relatively unaffected by human intervention.

When to visit, what to expect

The vast majority of visitors to these parks visit during the peak months of July and August. Inevitably, this places a great strain on the administration of the Parks, as well as leading to congestion on the roads, which were not built for such usage, and over-crowding at the popular sights. The canny park guest will always try and avoid this period, but for many, this is the only practical time when they can get there. Certainly, the weather will be at its most amenable during the summer months, but it is not necessarily the best time to see wildlife or enjoy the views.

The annual calendar for the parks can be seen in the following, general way:

Winter: November - May
Temperatures will be cold to very cold. Storms will be common with heavy falls of snow, and can last for several days. A fascinating time in the Parks, but precautions against the elements will be necessary.

Spring: May - June
Early season in the Parks. A good time to see wildlife with their young. Some facilities will not yet be open. Depending on the weather, some roads may still be blocked by snow.

Summer: July - August
A good time for activities such as water sports and hiking. The Park facilities will be in full swing. Hotels and campgrounds will be busy and possibly difficult to get into. Roads will be congested, and as this is the best time for road repairs, some may be temporarily closed. Many of the large mammals will have headed into the uplands during this period. Upland meadows in full flower. Warm days with cool nights. Occasional overnight frosts, and light snow falls not unusual.

Autumn: September - October
The best time to see wildlife as it descends from the uplands and the mating season begins. The Fall colors of the trees and the colder, crisper air make this a good time for seeing the Parks. The reduced crowds make the visit a pleasure, although some facilities will be winding down or closed for the season. More rain prevalent, with snow dusting the higher peaks. Autumn tints give the region a rich glow.

Bears, and Other Large Mammals

The bear is undoubtedly the most feared and at the same time, most loved of all the large mammals found in the USA. Rarely is any creature the subject of such extremes of human emotion, attraction and terror, and for the grizzly bear, that may indeed be its downfall.

In the Yellowstone Ecosystem, the black bear (*Ursus americana*) and the grizzly bear (*Ursus arctus horribilis*) roam freely. The black bear is by far the most numerous, although due to its usually timid nature, its population is difficult to estimate. The grizzly population, which has been heavily studied over the last 30 years, is believed to be around 300 bears.

The danger to the average park visitor from bears has unquestionable been overemphasized in some quarters, particularly in the media. While bears, especially the grizzly, pose a real danger to humans under certain circumstances, this risk is very small.

Anyone who visits these Parks should be aware of the bears, not only for their own safety and the safety of others, but also that they understand that their actions may ultimately affect the future of bears in the area. The less contact bears have with man the better. A much used phrase within the Parks is "*A Fed Bear Is A Dead Bear*".

Perhaps surprisingly, the bison probably represents a greater risk to visitors, particularly those who do not visit the backcountry areas. The bison is much underestimated by visitors. It appears to be slow and dull-witted, whereas in reality it can move very quickly and show its bad temper through goring humans who harass it. Elk and moose likewise, have injured and even killed humans who get too close. It is important for all Park visitors to respect the wildlife and not approach too closely. Some wildlife biologists suggest that if an animal such as a bison looks at you, then you are already too close, and he is in effect warning you to back off. Also, be aware that harassing animals is illegal, and this includes chasing them through the undergrowth for that one-in-a-million photograph. If you are taking photographs try to be unobtrusive. Photograph from behind a tree or from behind a vehicle, using it as a blind.

If you are intending to venture out into the backcountry, particularly in Yellowstone, there is a section on how to deal with the issue of bears in the backcountry camping section.

Backcountry Safety

If there was one thing the backcountry traveller could do to significantly reduce the risk of having an outing turn into a fight for survival, it is to adhere to the old rule - *Never Travel Alone.*

While this is undoubtedly good advice, it is not always realistic. Indeed some travellers, ourselves included, relish travelling alone through the backcountry as it seems to heighten the senses and makes one more aware of ones surroundings and the complex interplay of animals, plants and the geology.There are many ways to increase your safety in the wilderness, and most of these revolve around acquiring skills that enable you to avoid many of the possible pitfalls.

A key skill is the ability to read a map, and use a compass. Any fool can hold a compass out and tell you which direction is north. It takes experience to know how to take a bearing either from a map, or off natural features to determine ones position using triangulation.

Getting lost in the wilderness can be a frightening experience - it can also turn out fatal. Most of the trails in this book are relatively short and well-marked, at least in summer. If you venture out in the winter, bear in mind that trails become obscured and storms can roll in very quickly with stunning ferocity.

Here are some points that are worth remembering, whatever time of year you venture out:

• The weather can change very quickly and it can snow any time of the year.

• On the longer trails, always carry a few emergency supplies such as waterproof, spare clothing, torch, map & compass, energy foods and a whistle.

• Bears, elk, bison and moose all pose a potential threat if surprised or approached too closely. Treat them all with respect. Do anything you can to avoid disturbing them. In areas where bear activity, particularly grizzly, is high, travel in groups and consider wearing a bear bell or, better, shouting loudly.

• That strange grey crust that surrounds much of the geothermic features in the area can be as little as an eighth of an inch thick and may not support your weight. The water beneath can be as hot as 200 degrees fahrenheit. Exercise considerable caution when near geothermal areas, especially those that lack walkways. People have fallen through the crust and have died in the very hot waters. Don't let it happen to you.

• Areas that were severely burned in the 1988 fires in the Yellowstone National Park now present an additional hazard, that of falling trees. Since the fire, the dead trees, called snags, have deteriorated to such an extent that travel amongst them in windy weather could be hazardous.

• Know your limitations. Always be prepared to turn around and go back rather than push on regardless of weather, energy or fading light.

Environmental Considerations

No book advocating getting into the wilderness would be complete today without warnings about drinking the water and disposal of waste. The key to ensuring that the wilderness remains as pristine as possible, is to ensure that all trash that you take in comes out with you. This includes items once rarely thought of as litter, such as orange peel or cigarette butts. These items are not part of the Yellowstone Ecosystem and disfigure it for others.

This also means packing out human waste, however distasteful it may seem. The advent of self-sealing plastic bags makes this possible. If you cannot bring yourself to do this, then take a small trowel and dig a hole six inches deep, at least 100 feet from any water source, and cover it up afterwards. Do it well away from backcountry campsites. There is really no excuse for doing your business 10ft away from the trail or camp site, covering it with toilet paper, and then walking away.

The backcountry water sources within most, if not all, of the contiguous United States are now contaminated with various water-borne parasites and bacteria. The easiest way for a backcountry traveller to treat water is to boil it. This is still the simplest and one of the most effective methods. Opinion differs as to the length of boiling time required, but a couple of minutes is probably sufficient. There are also various water sterilizing tablets available, all seem to flavor the water somewhat. More recently there have come onto the market a range of water purifying devices which weigh little but can treat the water (with varying degrees of efficiency) without leaving a nasty taste.

Please avoid washing dishes or using any soap product in the rivers and streams. There are few more revolting sights than coming across an otherwise pristine creek to find pasta shells at the bottom.

If you must have a fire, use only the fire rings already established at the backcountry campsites. On occasion there will be complete bans on lighting fires in the backcountry due to high wildfire risk. Check with the Rangers. Park rules prohibit the collection of any timber that is standing, regardless of whether it is dead or alive. It is becoming increasingly obvious that allowing camp fires in the backcountry creates a disproportionate amount of damage to the area around the camp site. This is due to the creation of trails into the woodland as people search ever further out looking for windfall. Coupled with the fact there are still some who will happily cut down living trees regardless, makes it all the more likely that backcountry fires will be banned in the not too distant future.

Area Closures

Parts of both National Parks will be closed, or off-trail travel restricted, during periods of the year to protect wildlife and provide periods of solitude. These include the Hayden Valley and Gallatin Mountains in Yellowstone, and the winter closures of Willow Flats in Grand Teton. Check with the Ranger Stations for up to date information.

Key to maps and trails

GT Indicates that the feature is either in, or near, Grand Teton National Park.

YS Indicates that the feature is either in, or near, Yellowstone National Park.

P Parking

T Trailhead

Main trail   Side trail

Acknowledgements

As is usual with a project of this size, numerous people have helped with ideas, photos and constructive comments. We would like to thank the following for their valuable assistance:
Chuck Anderson, Doug Doyle, Frank Ewing, Greg Falk, Tracie Fifer, Babette Harding, David A. Hardison, Jeff Heilbrun, Rodney Lewis, Fred Lutz, Sharlene Milligan, Rod Newcomb, Jesse O'Connor, Andy Olpin, Tom Segerstrom, Lad Shunneson, Eric Soyland, Mark & Julie Springett, Frank Teasley, 'Troutie', Patti & Trevor Twose, Robert Weed, Jim Weeks, Dave Whaley, and the staff at Teton Mountaineering.
A special thanks goes to Dick DuMais for his assistance and encouragement.

July 4th Balloon Festival in Driggs, Idaho.

Photo: Patti Twose

BALLOONING

For the early morning types, a balloon ride is a great way to get a new perspective on the Tetons. Lighter-than-air travel is very peaceful, and even those who profess to be scared of heights, often find it more exhilarating than frightening.

The balloon you will travel in is usually about 8 stories high with a passenger capacity of 6 persons. These flying machines have precise vertical control, but are at the mercy of the winds for direction. A safe flying wind speed is considered to be up to about 8 miles per hour, so your ride will be a tranquil experience. From the point of view of safety, because of this requirement for good weather conditions, the sport of ballooning is relatively safe, and is, like all aviation, administered by the F.A.A. (Federal Aviation Authority). For this reason, there is always the possibility of the flight being cancelled at the last moment by the pilot for safety reasons. If you are determined to get a flight in the area during your stay, it may be a good idea to allow yourself several opportunities in case weather conditions are not favorable.

Customarily, a balloon ride starts early in the morning when the air is calm, with a average flight time of an hour. With the set-up and travel, you will need to allow about 3 hours for the whole trip. At this time of morning, the air will be chilly, so you are advised to dress warmly. Ballooning is a summer activity in this region.

For partners who do not wish to share the experience, it is sometimes possible for them to get a ride with the 'chase crew' who follow the balloon for recovery purposes.

For balloon buffs, or amateur photographers, there is the annual July 4th Hot Air Balloon Festival in Driggs, Idaho.

Lighter-than-air travel is an experience not to be missed.

For a list of ballooning companies operating in the Jackson Hole area, see the Reference Section at the back of the book.

Magpie and Golden Eagle in flight.

B I R D I N G

The diversity of the landscape in this region makes for a varied animal population, and this is reflected in a wide range of birds. For the amateur ornithologist, this is a good area for birding as some of the species are difficult to see elsewhere, yet reside in larger numbers here due to the limited impact of man.

We have chosen species for this list that should be identifiable to the layman without recourse to complicated identification books. A pair of binoculars will certainly make your life easier, but are not essential, and a note book is useful for jotting down observations. More essential to success will be patience and some preliminary groundwork to pick the most likely habitats to visit. For example, the Trumpeter Swan is often seen on the southern edge of the Elk Refuge, just north of Jackson, while the Osprey inhabits the Grand Canyon of the Yellowstone River.

Remember that you are entering their habitat. Birds tend to be more active between sunrise through to mid-morning. Approach your chosen area on foot, in an unhurried manner. Birds, like humans, do not appreciate being startled. Once you feel comfortable with your surroundings, relax and settle back for a few minutes. A stick-seat, folding chair or natural seat like a tree stump will make the wait more acceptable.

When identifying birds, size is quite important. The measurements given here are approximate, and refer to length from bill-tip to the end of the tail feathers. Note that coloring varies according to the sex of the bird, and the notes here are really very general. For more in depth information, a good bird-spotting book is an essential tool.

Molesting birds is illegal in the USA, as is taking eggs or the taking of any bird. Some of the birds listed here are endangered, and care should be taken to minimize your intrusion into their environment.

White Pelican *Pelicanus erythrorhynchos*

One of the big boys! A clever fisherman with the ability to work with others while swimming to encircle the fish, corralling them up for a feast. Youngsters are naked at birth and consequently must be shielded by their parents from the sun, otherwise they would die.

Identification:
54" - 70". Huge. White with black primaries. Large and distinctive yellow pouched bill.

Voice:
Virtually silent. Will utter a low groan when in colonies.

Habitat:
Lakes, marshland and shallow areas of water for fishing. Small islands, away from predators.

Nest:
Pair of whitish eggs. On ground, in amongst the reeds.

Summary:
A vanishing breed, due to insecticide poisoning. Do not disturb these birds during intense sunshine or at noon as they could be busy shielding their young from the sun.
Seen Spring through Fall.
Most likely location will be Yellowstone Lake.

Great Blue Heron   *Ardea herodias*

Tall and skinny, the Heron is a long-legged wading bird. A favorite pose seems to be standing motionless. Actually it is waiting for its next meal! Often nests high up in tall trees. Often mistaken for a crane. Can be distinguished from the crane by its neck - the crane flies with the neck outstretched, while the heron tucks it into a fold.

Identification:
42" - 52". Blackish with blue-gray wings. Some yellow on beak. White head with distinguished black stripe.

Voice:
A typical 'tall and silent type'. A loud croak - sounds like '*kraak*'.

Habitat:
Wetlands, especially favors areas with trees or rocky outcrops.

Nest:
Up to six blue/green eggs. Nest is made from twigs and small branches.

Summary:
Equally at home as a pair, or in large heronries with as many as 100 birds. Seen year round.
Most likely locations include the wetlands at the north end of Jackson Lake, and around Yellowstone Lake.

Canada Goose *Branta canadensis*

The Canada Goose is very much a creature of habit. Likes to return to its home ground year after year. Outside of the breeding season, its gregarious nature means it is often seen with others.

Identification:
22" - 45". Brown/grayish body. Black neck and head. A rather debonair bird with a distinctive white patch on the side of the head (almost looks like a chinstrap!).

Voice:
A rather noisy bird in flight, a nasal *'aa-honk'*.

Habitat:
Varied. Lakes, wetlands, rivers and even fields.

Nest:
4 - 8 large white eggs.

Summary:
The Canada Goose is protected as a rare and endangered species.
Seen year round.
Most likely locations include Jackson Lake and Yellowstone Lake, as well as Flat Creek north of Jackson.

Trumpeter Swan *Olor buccinator*

The largest bird listed here, and one of the biggest in North America. The Trumpeter Swan is an elegant bird with considerable poise.

Identification:

60" - 72". Snowy white. Black bill. Young have some coloring in their bill. On the water, note how the Trumpeter Swan keeps its neck vertical with it's bill parallel to the water.

Voice:

Loud booming, low-pitched *'ko-hoh'*.

Habitat:

Marshes, lakes and rivers with foliage.

Nest:

About 6 whitish eggs. Prefers to nest on islands with lots of reeds for cover.

Summary:

Once close to extinction, conservation efforts have helped to increase their numbers back into the thousands.

Seen year round.

Most likely locations include Yellowstone Lake and Flat Creek north of Jackson.

Bald Eagle *Haliaeetus levcocephalus*

A magnificent bird, the Bald Eagle is quite rare, and a treat to see in the wild. A member of the Hawk family.

Identification:
30" - 43". Large, dark brown body, white head and yellow bill. A snow white head indicates a bird of more than 5 years of age. Younger birds will have a darker head.

Voice:
Not what you might expect, it is actually a series of weak, thin cackling sounds.

Habitat:
Loves fish! Found near lakes and rivers.

Nest:
2 -4 buff colored blotchy eggs. Its nest - an eyrie - is used year after year and is located in trees or rocks.

Summary:
A scavenger by nature, it suffered from the use of pesticides. Illegal hunting has also diminished its numbers.
Seen year round.
Most likely locations include Oxbow Bend, just to the east of Jackson Lake Junction, and the Snake and Yellowstone Rivers.

Golden Eagle *Aquila chrysaetos*

Quite common in many of the Western States, the Golden Eagle is a bird of majesty and grace. A delight to see in the wild, the wing span is often the most remarkable feature when seen on the wing. Member of the Hawk family.

Identification:

30" - 40". Dark brown. White wing patch and tail bands can be seen clearly when in flight. Has a 'fanned' tail.

Voice:

Seldom heard! Sporadic mewing and high squeals.

Habitat:

Canyonlands and forested, mountainous regions.

Nest:

2 off-white, blotchy eggs. Nests on high rocky ledges or in trees.

Summary:

Contrary to popular belief, Golden Eagles rarely ever attack healthy livestock or large animals, unless the prey is old or injured.

Seen year round.

Try Garnet Canyon in Grand Teton National Park.

Osprey   *Pandion haliaetus*

The Osprey feeds exclusively on fish and consequently has the nickname 'Fish Eagle'. Member of the Hawk family.

Identification:

21"-24". Large. Brown above, white underparts. The Osprey haa a very distinctive 'band' on its wing which is seen while it is in flight.

Voice:

Loud whistles in general. When aroused or alarmed, it utters a '*ki-yewk ki-yewk*'.

Habitat:

Near lakes or rivers.

Nest:

2 - 4 buff colored, blotchy eggs. Nest is perched on a rocky outcrop or pole.

Summary:

Often seen near the Snake River and in the Grand Canyon of the Yellowstone River.

Seen Spring through Fall.

Swainson's Hawk   *Buteo swainsoni*

One of the more common members of the Hawk family. Migrates to South America during the winter. An expert of thermalling - the skill of riding warm air currents upwards - then leaving to glide down and repeat the process on another thermal.

Identification:

19" - 22". Dark brown above. White throat with dark bib.

Voice:

Largely silent. Sometimes whistles around the nest.

Habitat:

Plains and prairies.

Nest:

2-4 blueish white eggs. Uses a crude nest in a tree, or on a rock ledge or even on the ground.

Summary:

Often hunts on or from the ground. At migration time, one of the great sights is to see thousands heading off together going south.

Seen Spring through Fall.

Most likely to be seen in Jackson Hole.

American Kestrel *Falco sparverius*

Also known as the Sparrow Hawk, the American Kestrel is of the Falcon family. Not much larger than a House Sparrow! Often seen near highways, either perched on telephone wires, or hovering while searching for prey.

Identification:

8" - 12". Small. Pointed wings, unlike the 'fan' of larger birds of prey such as eagles. Blue/gray head. White underparts.

Voice:

A very loud and piercing '*killy killy killy*'.

Habitat:

From countryside to farm houses and even built-up areas.

Nest:

3-5 gray/white spotted eggs. Uses tree holes and abandoned nests of other species.

Summary:

Eats insects, and in particular grasshoppers, keeping them under control. Seen year round.

Most likely locations include Antelope Flats in Grand Teton.

Steller's Jay   *Cyanocitta stelleri*

A rather shy and silent type, often seems content to watch from a distance. The only western jay with a crested head.

Identification:

12" - 13". Black head crest and breast. Blueish above, and deep blue underneath.

Voice:

A harsh '*chook*' or '*shack*' sound repeated. Occasionally screeches.

Habitat:

Mainly forested areas.

Nest:

3-5 green, spotted eggs. Well camouflaged and constructed.

Summary:

A very distinctive blue color makes identification easy.

Seen year round.

Abundant, most visitors will see this bird while out hiking.

Black-billed Magpie *Pica pica*

The Black-billed Magpie has a special feature - its tail is longer than its body! A scavenger by nature, it can often be seen near dumpsters or anywhere where it can get a free meal.

Identification:
18" - 22". Large. Black head and front. Black bill and underneath. White belly and shoulder area.

Voice:
A quick nasal '*mag mag mag*' or '*chek chek chek*'.

Habitat:
Open land, brush land and small rivers.

Nest:
6-9 green, blotchy eggs in a well formed nest cup.

Summary:
They often share the region with fellow magpies.
Seen year round.
Abundant, particularly near habitation.

Gray Jay *Perisoreus canadensis*

A common sight in campgrounds, the Gray Jay is the original 'camp rob-ber' with unmatched opportunistic stealing skills.

Identification:

10" - 13". Dark gray above, light gray underneath. Dark neck, with white forehead and face.

Voice:

A whistling '*pwee-ah*'.

Habitat:

Forests.

Nest:

3-5 green/gray spotted eggs. Soft nest.

Summary:

Seen year round.

Abundant, throughout region.

Common Raven *Corvus corax*

Entirely black in color, the Common Raven is a very intelligent bird with good problem-solving skills. A member of the Crow family.

Identification:

21½" - 27". Large. Black all over. Wedge-shaped tail. Ruffled neck feathers.

Voice:

A rather hoarse croaking sound normally. When in flight it can produce a 'knocking' sound.

Habitat:

Varied.

Nest:

4-7 green, spotted eggs. It makes an eclectic nest of a variety of items, whatever it can find. Nests on cliffs or in trees.

Summary:

The Raven has the ability to soar like a hawk, rather than flapping its wings like a crow.

Seen year round.

Abundant, throughout the region.

Belted Kingfisher *Megaceryle alcyon*

Looking like it needs a haircut, the Belted Kingfisher really knows how to catch fish. Its favorite method is to perch on an isolated spot, sight its food (fish or insect), then cruise on over. At this point it hovers above the prey before a final headlong dive for the catch.

Identification:

11" - 14". Blueish gray above. Whitish underneath. White collar.

Voice:

A long coarse rattle.

Habitat:

Riverbanks and lake shores.

Nest:

5-8 white eggs. Nests in holes bored in stream banks.

Summary:

Seen year round.

Try the Snake and Yellowstone Rivers.

Broad-tailed Hummingbird *Selasphorus platycercus*

The Broad-tailed Hummingbird is philoptric by nature, meaning that it returns to the same branch year after year. It will even build its nest on top of the old one, if it is still there.

Identification:

4" - 4½". Medium sized. Metallic green above, white underneath. forked tail.

Voice:

A sharp *'chick'*.

Habitat:

Varied, wood and meadows.

Nest:

2 white eggs. Makes a woven nest if lichen and plant material.

Summary:

The adult males do a unique trick amongst hummingbirds, they produce a loud trilling with their wings when in flight.

Seen Spring through Fall.

Difficult to see, try the woodland area at Lupine Meadows, or String Lake.

Calliope Hummingbird *Stellula calliope*

North America's smallest hummingbird. Despite its size it can still fly with the best, as it winters in Mexico!

Identification:

2¾" - 4". Metallic green above. Throat is white with purple rays. This is actually a unique feature as all other North American Hummingbirds have solid green throats (technically known as *Gorget*).

Voice:

Light and even '*chip chip chip*'.

Habitat:

Varied. Upper meadows and forest glades.

Nest:

2 small white eggs.

Summary:

Whether defending a source of food or performing a mating display, this hummer will fly its very own flight path. Each species has its own unique pattern.

Seen Spring through Fall.

Again, difficult to see. Same likely locations as the Broad-tailed Hummingbird.

American Dipper *Cinclus mexicanus*

The 'Pavarotti' of waterbirds! The American Dipper revels in fast-flowing cold mountain streams. So much so that it sings with great aplomb. The only aquatic songbird in North America.

Identification:

7" - 8½". Slate gray. Long bill and stubby tail. Yellowish feet.

Voice:

Boisterous songsters, they can even out-sing the sounds of the river with their chipper trills.

Habitat:

Close to fast moving streams.

Nest:

3-6 white eggs. Roomy, well-insulated, stream-side dwelling.

Summary:

Happily plundering all forms of insect life, it plunges into the stream and feeds of insects and larvae it finds there.

Seen year round.

Most likely locations include fast flowing creeks throughout the area.

Great Horned Owl *Bubo virginianus*

One of the largest members of the Owl family. Has a most distinctive and familiar silhouette. His 'horns' are actually ear tufts. His ears are tucked away out of sight and are incredibly sensitive.

Identification:

18"-25". Large. Dark gray/brownish. Distinctive ear tufts.

Voice:

Typically a familiar '*hoo-hoo*' or '*twoo-twoo*'.

Habitat:

Varied, always with woodland nearby.

Nest:

2-3 white eggs. Usually uses abandoned nests of other birds.

Summary:

The 'stealth bomber' of the owl world. Like most owls the wings are 'feathered' and as a result do not catch the air, which would give an audible warning to its prey.

Seen year round.

Try the woodland areas near Taggart Lake and around Shoshone Lake.

Blue Grouse   *Dendragapus obscurus*

The Blue Grouse's claim to fame could be said to be its display of territory. The male climbs up on a higher perch than the ground and launches into an impressive vocal display.

Identification:

15"-21". Blueish gray. Sometimes dark gray. Males have a small amount of yellow/orange comb above the eye. Females are mottled brown with black-ish tails.

Voice:

Demonstrates a rich series of hoots and whoops, getting progressively loud-er and faster.

Habitat:

Forested areas, open slashes and clearings.

Nest:

5-10 buff colored eggs, lightly dotted. Nests in a depression in the ground.

Summary:

Feeds on berries, seeds and insects during the summer months, during the winter almost exclusively on pine needles.

Seen year round.

Try the woodland on the lower slopes of the Tetons, as well as the wood-land areas of Yellowstone.

Sage Grouse   *Centrocercus urophasianus*

The Sage Grouse gets its name from the fact that it lives on the sage brush. It even lives amongst it. Like the Blue Grouse, it gives a great display of ground territory, and courtship, with plenty of strutting and ruffled neck feathers.

Identification:
26"-30". Large. Grayish in color. Male is larger than the female.

Voice:
When flushed, or disturbed, gives out a '*cluck cluck cluck*'. During courtship, the male makes popping sounds. Females criss-cross males area squatting before males of their choice!

Habitat:
Sage brush.

Nest:
7-10 olive, lightly spotted eggs. Nests in well concealed grassy depression.

Summary:
For all the puffing of chests etc. during courtship, most males take more than one mate.

Seen year round.

Not surprisingly, seen in sagebrush. In Teton, try around the Antelope Flats area, and in Yellowstone, up near Bunsen Peak.

Mt. Moran & Jackson Lake from Signal Mountain Campground

C A M P I N G

Camping is THE way to visit the Yellowstone and Grand Teton National Parks. While there are hotels in both parks that provide very high standards of accommodation and culinary delights, they do not, in our opinion, reflect the true flavor of these wonderful parks.

The majority of the campgrounds are Park Service run, and in many ways, fairly basic. This is, however, part of their attraction. Some of the larger sites are run by concessionaires and as a result, have a wider range of facilities, including the somewhat hedonistic luxury of hot showers.

All the campgrounds in this region will be popular during the summer rush. We suggest that you arrive in the morning to grab your site, before embarking on the days activities. If they are already full, then there are plenty of campgrounds around the perimeters of both Parks that are just as good, albeit less well-placed for access. The Visitors Centers in the Parks will have suggestions for alternative sites nearby. Some of the best sites are run by the Forest Service in the National Forests. The Bridger Teton National Forest has a Visitors Center in the town of Jackson. There are also plenty of private sites, some better than others.

When you enter the campgrounds, you will be reminded to keep a clean camp while camping. Whether you are using a RV, truck or tent, the safeguards are not only for you, but also those who come after you. Note that the campground hosts will enforce clean camp rules, and fines will be levied if you do not adhere to them.

While camping in the organized campgrounds in the parks, particularly in Yellowstone, don't lose too much sleep worrying about bears coming into the campground. Providing you have kept a clean area, and not taken food into your tent, you are very unlikely to have problems with bears. If you are camping in the backcountry, make sure you reserve your site before setting out, and pay attention to all regulations regarding bears.

General Camping Information - Yellowstone

1.   All opening dates given for campgrounds were for the 1994 season. Check with the Park Service before setting out for current opening dates. Due to weather conditions and resource management, the Park Service may need to close sites at short notice, or open them later than expected. Similarly, the site fees are subject to change.

2.   Camping outside of these sites or allocated backcountry sites is prohibited. This includes pullouts, picnic areas and those quiet little spots that you think no one will notice if you come back later in the evening!

3.   Between June 15th and Labor Day, there is a 14 night limit at any site. The limit is 30 days for the rest of the year.

4.   2 sites, Canyon and Fishing Bridge, are run by T.W. Recreation Services. They can be contacted at T.W. Recreational Services, Yellowstone National Park, WY 82190. Tel: (307) 344-7311.

5.   Check out time at all campgrounds is 10.00am.

6.   Shower and laundry facilities are available at the following locations: Canyon Village Campground, Fishing Bridge RV Park, Grant Village Campground, Lake Lodge *(laundry only)*, Old Faithful Lodge *(showers only)*.

1.   Tower Falls   `YS`

Sites: 32	Fee: $6
Run by: Park Service	**Stay limit:** 14 days
Open: May 21 - Sept 13	**Reservations:** No

Comments: RV's ok. No hookups. Fire grates. Pit toilets. Tower Fall is a quiet little site, but very popular and getting a site can be difficult. There is a store nearby at the pull-in for the Falls. Roosevelt Lodge is a couple of miles up the road where there is a restaurant with a good family menu, as well as a gas station.

Tower Falls is located 19 miles north of Canyon Village and 18 miles east of Mammoth Hot Springs where a wider range of facilities are available.

The Falls can be reached by a trail the other side of the main highway. If you continue downstream from the Falls for about ¼ mile, following Tower Creek, you come to the Yellowstone River and Bannock Ford. This is the only convenient river crossing in this part of the region and figured prominently in early Yellowstone history.

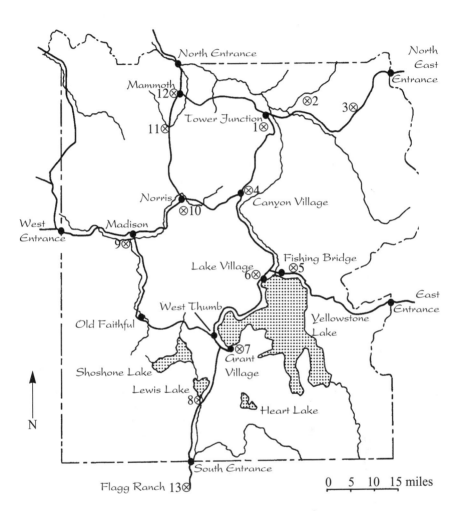

Yellowstone Campgrounds

1. Tower Falls
2. Slough Creek
3. Pebble Creek
4. Canyon
5. Fishing Bridge RV Park
6. Bridge Bay
7. Grant Village
8. Lewis Lake
9. Madison
10. Norris
11. Indian Creek
12. Mammoth
13. Flagg Ranch

2.   Slough Creek   YS

Sites: 29	Fee: $6
Run by: Park Service	Stay limit: 14 days
Open: May 21 - Nov 1	Reservations: No

Comments: RV's ok. No hookups. Fire grates. Pit toilets. Good fishing in the adjacent Slough Creek. Probably one of the park's best campgrounds, it is feels more remote than the others. A good spot for hikers and fishermen. The nearest facilities are at Roosevelt Lodge some 7 miles away, with a full range of services at Mammoth Hot Springs, some 25 miles east.

For wildlife enthusiasts, there is good elk and bison viewing possible just down the main highway west towards Tower Junction.

If you head east on the main highway towards Cooke City for about 4 miles there is the Specimen Ridge Exhibit. This is one of the most extensive fossilized forest areas to be found anywhere and is well worth a visit. Volcanic ash covered forest here on numerous occasions, burying the trees so that now, after erosion has revealed them, they can be seen.

3.   Pebble Creek   YS

Sites: 36	Fee: $6
Run by: Park Service	Stay limit: 14 days
Open: June 11 - Sept 7	Reservations: No

Comments: RV's ok. No hookups. Fire grates. Pit toilets. Not a particularly attractive site, it can feel rather cramped during the height of the summer rush.

Driving 4 miles north, the road travels through Icebox Canyon. This is a deep, narrow gorge, dark and brooding, which holds ice well into the summer months.

South of the campground is Trout Lake and Buck Lake on the west side of the road. Further south is Soda Butte, a travertine mound formed by a small hot spring that is notable for its isolation from other such features. On the east side of the road it is possible to see bison.

4. Canyon `YS`

Sites: 280	**Fee:** $8
Run by: T.W. Services	**Stay limit:** 14 days
Open: June 4 - Sept 7	**Reservations:** No

Note: Sites are allocated to newcomers - you are not supposed to just drive in and select a site before paying.
Comments: RV's ok. No hookups. Fire grates. Canyon is a big site buried fairly successfully in a heavily wooded area. On the plus side there are showers, and laundry facilities, as well as grocery stores and restaurants nearby. On the downside, it is very popular, and on some mornings in the summer you may have to wait more than an hour to get a vacated site. (If it was wet or cold the night before making the current residents tardy risers, you may even have to wait even longer!).

South from Canyon towards Yellowstone Lake is the Hayden Valley. Named after Ferdinand Hayden, one of the early surveyors of the region, it is a major habitat for bison, grizzly, elk and waterfowl.

5. Fishing Bridge RV Park `YS`

Sites: 345	**Fee:** $19
Run by: T.W. Services	**Stay limit:** 14 days
Open: May - Oct	**Reservations:** No

Comments: RV's only. All sites have hookups. Fire grates. Showers.
Note: Campground is open to hard-sided camping units only. Tents and tent-trailers are not allowed.

Possibly one of the most controversial campgrounds in the National Park system, the Fishing Bridge complex was built in the 1920's in what was then, and still is, prime grizzly habitat. Some steps have been taken to reduce the impact of so many people in this important area, including the creation of the Grant Village complex (itself in an important ecological location and therefore controversial) to replace it. The site is rather an eyesore, despite being in one of the most attractive parts of the Park. Its popularity is sufficient evidence that the conflict between the parks large mammals and its visitors, will continue for some time to come.

Despite its name, no fishing is allowed at Fishing Bridge.

Ah, for the endless summer!

6. Bridge Bay

`YS`

Sites: 420	**Fee:** $10
Run by: Park Service	**Stay limit:** 14 days
Open: May 21 - Sept 27	**Reservations:** Yes

Comments: This is the biggest and busiest campground in the Park. Set in woodland near the lake shore. RV's ok. No hookups. Flush toilets. Fire grates. Hot water. Showers and laundry facilities located 4 miles away at Fishing Bridge. Boat facilities include lake access, a marina and boat rental.

Gull Point is a prominent nearby picnic area out to the east beyond Bridge Bay.

Just a mile north is an area of the lake shore that offers good waterfowl viewing possibilities. There are also the well-known 'fish traps'. These are actually a stretch of rocks that extend out into the lake that may have been built by Indians to allow the catching of fish.

Reservations for Bridge Bay must be made through the Mistix reservation system. Call 1-800-365-2267. Outside of USA, call (619) 452-5956.

7. Grant Village

`YS`

Sites: 414	**Fee:** $8
Run by: Park Service	**Stay limit:** 14 days
Open: June 22 - Oct 11	**Reservations:** No

Comments: An unremarkable site, although the nearby facilities and the lake make it a popular destination. RV's ok. No hookups. Showers and laundry facilities just outside the campground. Fire grates. Boat launching facilities available nearby.

Due to bears being attracted to the spawning trout in the Big Thumb Creek inlet to Yellowstone Lake which is nearby, the season opening of this site is dependent upon the presence of the bears. Once the spawn is over, and the bears have moved on, the campground is opened.

One of the newest campgrounds in the Park, Grant Village was built in the 1970's to replace the controversial Fishing Bridge site. Even so, the placing of Grant Village drew fire itself due to its proximity to the spawning grounds that are so important to the bears. Ironically, Fishing Bridge is still open, and there are now two campgrounds in sensitive locations.

8. Lewis Lake   YS

Sites: 85	Fee: $6
Run by: Park Service	Stay limit: 14 days
Open: June 11 - Nov 1	Reservations: No

Comments: RV's ok. No hookups. Fire grates. Pit toilets. Boat launching facilities at the north end of the campground. One of the quietest sites in the Park - many visitors entering from the south seem to rush straight past on their way to the larger, better equipped sites at Grant Village and Bridge Bay. A good site for lake access and exploring the southern section of the Park. The nearest facilities, including showers and stores, are at Grant Village some 22 miles away.

Lewis Lake is the third largest lake in Yellowstone Park and is a good area for waterfowl viewing.

9. Madison   YS

Sites: 292	Fee: $8
Run by: Park Service	Stay limit: 14 days
Open: May 1 - Nov 1	Reservations: No

Note: Sites are allocated to newcomers - you are not supposed to just drive in and select a site before paying.

Comments: RV's ok. No hookups. Flush toilets. Another large site, Madison is located in a partly wooded area overlooked by Park Mountain. Some mornings you may be woken by the sound of a herd of bison passing through down near the river. There are no facilities in Madison, the nearest within the park being at Old Faithful, 16 miles away.

Driving west from Madison towards the West Entrance to the Park will take you through Madison Canyon, and along the Madison River. Elk, bison and waterfowl abound, as do fish.

South from Madison is Firehole Canyon Drive which follows an old section of the road along the Firehole River. The Firehole Falls is along here, and it is a pleasant little drive.

Mammoth Campground.

10. Norris

YS

Sites: 116	**Fee:** $8
Run by: Park Service	**Stay limit:** 14 days
Open: May 14 - Sept 27	**Reservations:** No

Comments: RV's ok. Flush toilets. No hookups. This partly wooded site overlooks the Gibbon River, and therefore a good location for fishermen. For non-fishermen, there is the nearby Norris Geyser Basin. There are no facilities in Norris - the nearest being at Canyon Village, about 12 miles away.

The Norris Geyser Basin is the most active geyser basin in the Park, and also the hottest. It is the home of Steamboat Geyser, the worlds tallest geyser. Steamboat Geyser has reached a height of more than 300ft. It is however, very unpredictable, having erupted only twice since 1990. More predictable is Echinus Geyser that erupts every 35-75 minutes and is fun to watch as it has a predictable preparation cycle prior to erupting.

11. Indian Creek

YS

Sites: 74	**Fee:** $6
Run by: Park Service	**Stay limit:** 14 days
Open: June 4 - Sept 13	**Reservations:** No

Comments: RV's ok, with maximum length of 45ft. No hookups. Fire grates. Pit toilets. Indian Creek is an attractive, mostly level site near the Gardner River. There are sites specifically for cyclists and hikers and the same for bikers. These have bear-proof storage lockers as well. The nearest store is at Mammoth, about 6 miles away. There is good fishing in the Gardner River nearby and it is well-placed for wildlife viewing in the area.

About 5 miles south of Indian Creek are the Obsidian Cliffs. Obsidian is a dark, glassy volcanic rock formed by the very rapid cooling of lava. Prized by the Indians, it forms sharp edges that can be used for cutting tools and projectile points. It is possible to approach the cliffs, but note that taking specimens of the obsidian is illegal.

12. Mammoth

Sites: 85	**Fee:** $8
Run by: Park Service	**Stay limit:** 14 days
Open: Year round	**Reservations:** No

Comments: Set on a largely open hillside facing east, the Mammoth site is very popular. The lack of trees make it rather hot during the height of summer. RV's ok. Flush toilets. No hookups. The site is within walking distance of Mammoth and all the services there, as well as the Mammoth Hot Springs. For inexpensive fast food, try the Terrace Grill in Mammoth.

Mammoth is the Park Headquarters and site of the old Fort Yellowstone. The town even today has the air of a military fort with many of the original of stone buildings. It was from here that the U.S. Cavalry ran the Park between 1886 and 1916 until the creation of the National Park Service.

Mammoth is substantially lower than the rest of the Park and as a result, has less severe weather during the winter months. This allows the campground to stay open year round. The warmer weather also attract elk who winter in the town.

13. Flagg Ranch

YS

Sites: 121	**Fee:** $14 tents, $19 RV's
Run by: Flagg Ranch	**Stay limit:** N/A
Open: June - September	**Reservations:** Yes

Comments: RV's ok, full hookups available. Showers and launderette. Facilities at the Ranch include motel rooms, cabins, restaurant and snack bar, grocery store and gasoline.

Flagg Ranch is also open during the winter from mid-December through mid-March.

For more information, call (307) 543-2861, or 1-800-443-2311, or write to Box 187, Moran, WY 83013.

Flagg Ranch is not actually in either Park. It lies within the John D. Rockefeller, Jr., Memorial Parkway that forms a corridor connecting the Parks. Its position makes it a good base for visiting both. A major center, it is also open during the winter months, and is the jump-off for snowcoach trips into Yellowstone from the south.

General Camping Information - Grand Teton

1.   All opening dates given for campgrounds were for the 1994 season. Check with the Park Service before setting out for current opening dates. Due to weather conditions and resource management, the Park Service may need to close sites at short notice, or open them later than expected. Similarly, the site fees are subject to change.

2.   Camping is not permitted at the roadside, or in the pullouts or picnic areas.

3.   Maximum length of stay in the campgrounds is 14 days (7 days at Jenny Lake Campground).

4.   Camping is first-come, first-served. The only exception to this is the concessionaire-run Colter Bay Trailer Village.

5.   Public showers and laundry facilities are available at Colter Bay Village. Open between May and October.

6.   Check out time is 10.00am.

14. Lizard Creek   `GT`

Sites: 62	**Fee:** $8
Run by: Park Service	**Stay limit:** 14 days
Open: June 12 - Sept 7	**Reservations:** No

Comments: No RV's longer than 25ft in length. No hookup's. Firegrates. One of the more aesthetically pleasing sites within the park and while most the sites lack a view, they are attractive due to their seclusion. The sites nearer the lake offer the best views of the lake and an end-on view of the Tetons. There are several walk-in sites, as well as the more common drive-up type. The proximity to the lake makes for good bird watching and fishing, but also provides a fine habitat for the mosquitoes! Nearest facilities are either Flagg Ranch or Colter Bay (8 miles). Can be full in summer by 2pm.

Incidentally, there are no lizards here. It appears that the name stems from early visitors seeing salamanders, that while looking similar to lizards, are in fact very different. The lizard lives on land, the salamander lives in water.

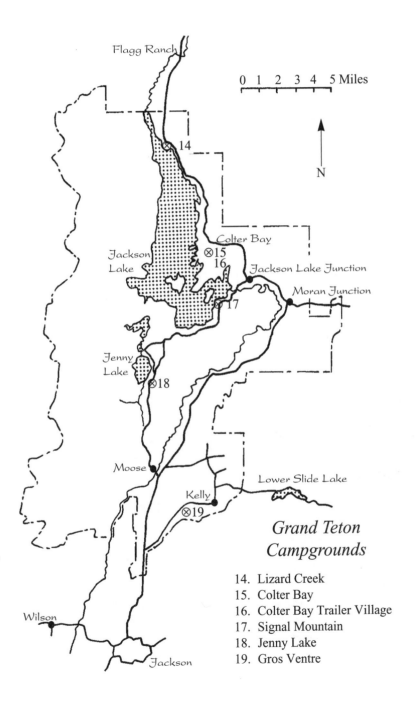

Flagg Ranch

0 1 2 3 4 5 Miles

N

⊗14

Colter Bay

Jackson
Lake

⊗15
16

Jackson Lake Junction

Moran Junction

⊗17

Jenny
Lake

⊗18

Moose

Lower Slide Lake

Kelly

⊗19

Wilson

Jackson

*Grand Teton
Campgrounds*

14. Lizard Creek
15. Colter Bay
16. Colter Bay Trailer Village
17. Signal Mountain
18. Jenny Lake
19. Gros Ventre

Signal Mountain Campground.

15. Colter Bay   `GT`

Sites: 310	**Fee:** $8
Run by: Park Service	**Stay limit:** 14 days
Open: May 15 - Sept 27	**Reservations:** No

Comments: A large, and somewhat bland site. RV's ok. No hookups. Firegrates. Showers. A good location with facilities, it is offset somewhat by being noisy and busy. There is boat access to the lake. During the main summer months it can fill by noon.

There are a number of short hiking trails around here, that are especially suitable for early evening strolls. A brochure describing the trails is available from the Visitor Center.

The whole of this area is a popular waterfowl spotting area, with good opportunities for seeing Trumpeter Swans and Sandhill Cranes. Moose also inhabit the wetlands and can often be seen early in the morning or at dusk.

16. Colter Bay Trailer Village   `GT`

Sites: 112	**Fee:** $21
Run by: Grand Teton Lodge Co.	**Stay limit:** N/A
Open: Mid May - Oct	**Reservations:** Yes

Comments: All sites are for RV's and all have hookups. Showers and launderette. Good lake access. A big and busy site, aesthetically bland, it is definitely not a wilderness experience. Good facilities in the village include a gas station, restaurant and stores. Reservations highly recommended during height of summer.

For reservations call (307) 543-2855 or write to The Grand Teton Lodge Company, Box 240, Moran, WY 83013.

17. Signal Mountain   `GT`

Sites: 86	**Fee:** $8
Run by: Park Service	**Stay limit:** 14 days
Open: May 8 - Oct 12	**Reservations:** No

Comments: On a wooded hillside overlooking Jackson Lake with Mt Moran in the distance. Some of the sites feel rather 'tight' to their neighbors but in general it is a spacious site. Can be busy and noisy during the hours of 8am-10am as it fills up, then can be quiet, the peace broken only by boats on the lake. There is a pleasant picnic area by the lake. A nightly Amphitheater talks program is provided by the Park Service. RV's ok. No hookups. Firegrates. No showers. Boat access to the lake.

Worthy of a visit is Signal Mountain itself. The summit, at 7,593ft, gives an elevated view of the whole valley, as well as a view east of the Bridger-Teton National Forest. Fortunately for the less-energetic, it is possible to drive to the summit.

Jenny Lake Campground.

18. Jenny Lake

Sites: 50	Fee: $8 ($2 for cyclists)
Run by: Park Service	Stay limit: 7 days
Open: May 22 - Sept 27	Reservations: No

Comments: Tents only. Firegrates. A quiet site, wooded and dominated by Teewinot and Cascade Canyon. A good central position and nearby fine walks make this a very popular site. There are also sites available just for cyclists with racks to lock up your bikes. This site has some of the most desirable camping 'real estate' in the park and can fill by mid-morning in the summer.

Jenny Lake is an excellent base for hiking in the Park, with several fine day hikes accessible nearby. Just south of the lake is Lupine Meadows which is the most popular start for climbers on their way up onto the Grand Teton. Even a short hike partway up towards Garnet Canyon can be rewarding experience with possibilities of seeing a variety of wildlife and flowers. During the Fall, Black Bears can be seen around here feeding on berries as they build up body fat in preparation for the long winter ahead.

19. Gros Ventre

Sites: 372	Fee: $8
Run by: Park Service	Stay limit: 14 days
Open: May 1 - Oct 12	Reservations: No

Comments: Isolated somewhat from the main section of the Park and this is for some a plus, for others an inconvenience. RV's ok. No hookups. Firegrates. No showers. Site lacks a clear view of the Tetons, unlike most of the other sites, although it is still a pleasant campground, dominated by Blacktail Butte. Sites are placed around the cottonwoods. It is possible to see wildlife. There is a tent-only section on north side. Doesn't often fill up. General store at Kelly which is 2 miles away. An Amphitheater Program provides nightly talks by the Park Rangers on a range of topics.

The nearby town of Kelly was wiped out when the lake formed by the slide of Gros Ventre burst its natural dam and washed through, sweeping all before it. On that day, May 18th 1927, six people were killed and the flood continued on right across the valley as far as Wilson.

At Kelly there is also the Kelly Warm Spring which is open for public swimming.

Backcountry camping - Summary of Regulations

Some visitors may be shocked at the number of regulations relating to backcountry camping within Yellowstone and Grand Teton National Parks. For a number of reasons, these have been increasing in recent years. The main reasons being impact on the sites due to overuse/abuse and the impact of the use of the sites on the wildlife within the Parks. Before getting too hot under the collar about these regulations, do bear in mind that they do go a long way towards ensuring that the visitor has a enjoyable experience. Without the reservation system, popular areas like Shoshone Lake in Yellowstone for instance, would be very busy indeed during the height of summer.

Backcountry sites may be closed at any time due to resource management requirements, in effect bear movements, nearby. The Ranger Station will notify you if this is the case.

These are only a summary of the regulations. More detailed information is available at the Backcountry offices.

1.   A Backcountry Permit is required for all use of backcountry sites. These are free and must be obtained no more than 48 hours in advance at a Backcountry Office. These are located at the Ranger Stations at Old Faithful, Mammoth, Canyon, Grant Village and Bechler for Yellowstone, and at the Moose or Colter bay Visitor Centers, or the Jenny Lake Ranger Station for Grand Teton.

2.   Camping outside of designated areas is prohibited.

3.   Open fires are only allowed at designated sites, and within established fire rings.

4.   Food must be suspended 10ft above the ground and 4ft horizontally away from the pole or tree.

5.   All trash must be packed out.

6.   Wheeled vehicles including bicycles are not allowed off designated trails.

7.   Human body waste must be disposed of more than 100ft away from water sources, campsites, and trails. Where pit toilets are provided, they should be used.

8.   Weapons, traps or nets are prohibited.

9.   Pets are prohibited in the backcountry.

Bears - Avoidance & Encounters

Backcountry camping is a very enjoyable experience, perhaps one of the finest experiences one can have in the area. Some simple precautions should make for a more enjoyable trip, and reduce the risk of having a close encounter of a bear kind.

Note: Bears are as unique and unpredictable as humans, and the advice given here is a summary of the best advice available. No one can guarantee your safety in the backcountry.

While hiking

Large parties are less likely to meet a bear due to the increased noise they make. If contact is made, a large party will be more intimidating, and therefore less likely to be charged.

Make noise while walking - shouting is probably the best bear scarer.

Don't hike at night unless in a dire emergency. If you have to, make a **lot** of noise, and use a flashlight.

If you smell rotting flesh then you are likely near a carcass of prey that may be guarded by a bear. Back-up and return the way you have come. Bears can be very protective of their food.

Avoid carrying smelly foods that may attract bears.

Identifying Bears.

If you sight a bear

The best course of action is to turn around and go back. If this is not feasible, then either detour, or wait for the bear to leave the area.

If the bear starts approaching you, and has not yet seen you, back up and try to find a tree to climb. Climb at least 15ft up. If this is not feasible, and the bear is still some distance away then it may be wise to make your presence known by shouting at the bear. This is a risky strategy however, as the bear may be startled and may charge. Bears have differing temperaments, and some may charge from further away than others. Alternatively, react as though the bear has charged (see below).

If a bear charges you

Hold your ground. Do not under any circumstances run, as the bear may give chase and you will not be able to outrun it. (The maximum speed of even the best athletes has never exceeded 28mph, while a bear can do an impressive 40mph over short distances).

Back up very slowly. If you have something you can drop to distract the bears attention, then do it. Do not drop food however, as the bear will learn that this is a way of getting fed.

Many bear charges are actually bluffs, and the bear will break off at the last moment. If it doesn't then drop to the ground and play dead. In the vast majority of bear attacks, it appears that the bear has reacted to a perceived threat and if you n longer seem to be a threat, then it is likely the bear will leave. For this reason, do not resist the attack. While on the ground, roll up, cover your neck and head with your arms, and protect your stomach with your legs. A rucksack will help protect your back.

Attacks at night

A bear that enters a campsite at night and attacks you in your tent is likely viewing you as prey. Under these circumstances, many experts consider that the best course of action is to fight back. If the bear does view you as prey, then feigning dead may be exactly the wrong course of action. It is important to note that there is no single course of action that guarantees your survival under these, admittedly extremely rare, circumstances.

Remember, bear attacks are extremely rare, and even in instances of man/bear contact, in most cases both parties leave unscathed.

Backcountry camping & bears

The risk from bears entering your camping area can be considerably reduced by following these simple guidelines:
• Make sure all food is stored in the correct manner, using a suspension system as noted overleaf.
• Any other odorous items such as lipsalve, toothpaste and candy should also be stored with the food.
• Wash all pans clean immediately after eating, and keep all pans well away from the tent.
• Cook all food in an area away from the tent.
• Take food that is not very odorous - such as dried meals.
• It is a good idea store clothes worn while cooking with the food, rather than keep them in your tent.
• Watch for food scraps being thrown away after the washing of dishes.
• Camp away from trails as bears make use of trails while travelling at night.
• Do not try and burn uneaten food in the fire pit unless the fire is hot enough to completely destroy it.

General Camp Etiquette
• Try to leave your campsite as you would like to find it.
• Use the pit toilet if there is one. Otherwise go some distance from the site.
• If you have an open fire, make sure it is fully out before leaving.
• Respect other campers right to privacy. Some backcountry sites may be nearby, and the residents may not welcome intrusion into their camp.

Bear-proof storage boxes at Leigh Lake

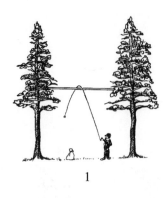

Horizontal Bear Pole

1

2

Storing food

Horizontal bear pole

Many backcountry campsites in the region have a single horizontal pole linking two trees. This system is the easiest to use. Tie a small branch or other heavy item to your length of rope and throw over the pole. Hoist your food bag up so that it is suspended more than 10ft above the ground, and at least four feet from either tree. Tie the rope off at one of the trees.

Vertical Bear Pole & storage containers

Some sites, particularly some of the boating sites around the smaller lakes in Grand Teton have bear-proof storage containers and poles. The poles are simple to use. There should be a hoisting pole nearby which is used to lift your bag up to be hooked by one of the hooks at the top of the pole.

The storage containers are likewise simple to use.

1

Two Trees Method

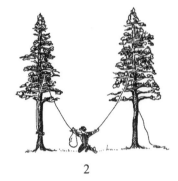

2

3

Two trees method

If your site does not have either of the systems available, this is the easiest way to store your food. Find two trees about 20ft apart and throw each end over a branch at least 15ft above the ground. Tie your bag to the middle of the cord and hoist up so that it is suspended midway between the trees. Tie off both ends.

All official backcountry campgrounds within these parks have trees nearby that can be used for this purpose.

If for any reason you are forced to make an emergency overnight stop away from a backcountry campground, store all food as discussed above. In the unlikely circumstance that there are no suitable trees nearby, then you will need to locate your food stashes some distance away from where you sleep. On no account should you keep it with you.

A typical scene at Biscuit Basin in winter.

CROSS-COUNTRY SKIING

Winter is a magical time of year to visit Yellowstone and Grand Teton National Parks, as increasing numbers of visitors are finding out. There are few experiences that can compare to a frosty clear morning in the shadows of the Tetons, skiing one of the many trails with the Tetons themselves as a backdrop. In Yellowstone, there is something special about seeing the geothermic features billowing clouds of steam with elk and bison nearby using the warmth.

However, despite the beauty of the scene, it is important to keep in mind that this is a potentially hostile environment. Blizzards can blow up very quickly and stay for days. The backcountry is no place to be caught unawares in bad weather. Rescue can be many hours away, and even the most trivial of problems can assume serious proportions when you are so isolated. Therefore, we strongly caution anyone heading into the backcountry to follow the simple guidelines given overleaf. Nothing can guarantee your safety in this wilderness, but these precautions will go a long way to reducing the danger.

The trails listed here within Yellowstone National Park all start from the Old Faithful area. During the winter months, the only practical way to get into this area is either by snowcoach, or by snowmobile. These services run from mid-December through to mid-March. Even though the snow will still allow skiing in Yellowstone into May, the Park effectively closes from mid-March through mid-May (varying year to year according to conditions). This is in part due to it being a very difficult time for the animals in the Park. Bears are just emerging from hibernation with their young and they need this time to build up strength without having to worry about humans. All the large mammals that have weathered the winter in the Park will be weak from the struggle against the elements. It is possible to make your own way into the Park on skis at this time of year, but you might want to consider whether your intrusion may not be good for the Park's inhabitants.

Winter Backcountry Safety

Winter checklist

Every member of your party should carry the following:

Water	High energy snack food	Layered clothing
Hat & gloves	Sunscreen and sunglasses	Map and compass
Spare clothing	Extra food	Ski spares kit
Headlamp	Watch	Fire starting materials
Whistle	Ski waxes and scraper	Tools and repair tape
Space blanket	Avalanche shovel	Avalanche transceiver or beacon.

A flask of hot coffee is a luxury that is well worth carrying.

Avalanches

"Avoiding avalanches is easier than surviving them."

The Avalanche Book. Betsy R. Armstrong & Knox Williams.

Avalanches are a fact of life in the mountains in winter, and if you venture out into them, you should be aware of the dangers from avalanches. There is no lack of information on the subject and we recommend the above book as a starter. There are also a number of Institutes and organizations that run Avalanche Clinics. You are urged to learn as much as you can on the subject as it may one day save your life.

Many writers on backcountry skiing recommend that all parties have a avalanche shovel and beacon per person. While we would not disagree with this viewpoint, it is essential to know how to use them.

For local avalanche conditions, contact the nearest Visitor Center, or call the Avalanche Hazard & Weather Forecast at (307) 733-2664. Also Teton Mountaineering in Jackson have up to date information, call (307) 733-3595.

Any avalanche report is, however, no substitute for your own, informed, on-site observations.

General safety rules and hints

Never travel alone.

Be careful when skiing on frozen lakes. There may be hidden hazards.

Let someone know where you are going and when you are due to return.

Sign in at the trailhead register.

Do not overestimate your abilities, or underestimate the outing.

Pack out all trash.

Take care when skiing around thermal features, and give them a wide berth.

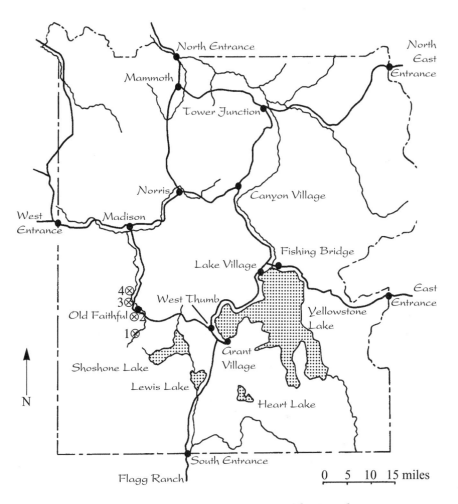

Yellowstone Cross-Country Ski Trails

1. Lone Star Geyser
2. Fern Cascades
3. Upper Geyser Basin & Biscuit Basin
4. Fairy Falls

1.   Lone Star Geyser   `YS`

Distance: 8 miles	**Difficulty:** Moderate
Time Required: Half day	**Terrain:** Good trails, well marked
Start elevation: 7,360ft	**Elevation gain:** 300ft
Best time of year: Mid-December to mid-March	

A good introduction to one of the harder tours in the Park. It is comparatively long compared to many of the trails listed here, but offers interesting scenery in a remote setting. While mainly flat, the Howard Eaton Trail has a fairly short, steep descent that the beginner may want to avoid by going in the opposite direction to the one described here, or returning via the old road.

From the Old Faithful Snow Lodge (note sign for Lone Star Geyser and Mallard Lakes) head north-east around the parking lot to the old road which heads down to the bridge over the Firehole River. Just beyond there is a trail junction. Mallard Lakes is to the left, Lone Star Geyser to the right. Go right. The trail climbs gradually uphill for ½ mile to almost reach the Grand Loop Road.

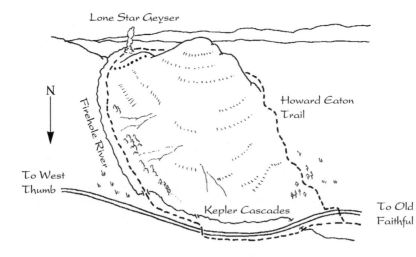

Skiers at Lone Star Geyser.

Photo: R. DuMais

The trail then parallels the road for a mile, to finally cross the road at the Kepler Cascades. Here a wooden platform jutting out over the canyon gives a good view of the Falls.

The trail heads east from here, along the side of the river for a short distance to the Lone Star Geyser Road. Ski this road as it heads south. The road is level much of the way as it follows the course of the Firehole River. The road ends after 2 miles at a clearing with the Lone Star Geyser. The geyser currently erupts every 3 hours or so. The open slopes around here make a good lunch spot on a sunny day.

Beyond the geyser, the trail curls around the base of the hillside and through woods to join the Howard Eaton Trail. The trail is well marked with blazes to keep you on course. Go straight ahead here (the right branch will take you back to the Lone Star Geyser road and a flatter return to the start). The trail heads through woodland and gently climbs up to the flat top of higher ground. A section of zigzags leads steeply, and in icy conditions rather quickly, back down to Old Faithful. This is a fine section in good conditions.

At the end of the downhill it meets the Fern Cascades loop, close to the main highway. Cross the road and ski on to return to the Old Faithful area.

2.   Fern Cascades

Distance: 3 miles   **Difficulty:** Moderate
Time Required: 2 hours   **Terrain:**   Rolling woodland
Start elevation: 7,360ft   **Elevation gain:** 250ft
Best time of year: mid-December - mid-March

This trail is a short loop that stays close to the Old Faithful area. Good in either direction, going the way described the buildings at the complex are soon left behind, and the trail finishes with a good downhill section.

From the Snow Lodge, go south past the ski shop and Snowshoe Lodge (signs) and cross the entrance road and the Grand Loop Road. Ski to the junction with the Howard Eaton Trail and the start of the Fern Cascades loop. Go right (west) past powerlines and on past a housing and utility area. Follow the arrows and blazes for a few hundred yards, then left past houses to the bottom of the hillside. The trail through this section seems confusing but in fact it is well blazed and should not present any route finding problems. Climb up

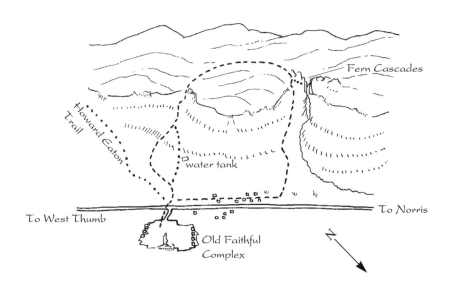

Since 1988, you can see the wood for the trees!
Photo: R. DuMais

(south) along a steep hillside through burned lodgepole pine forest. Then less steeply as the hillside is traversed as it heads towards Spring Creek and a sign for Fern Cascades. Be careful about getting too far out onto steep hillsides in an attempt to see the Falls.

The trail then goes east, over the broad, flat, crest of a ridge through trees and clearings. The trail wanders in here. A gradual decent to the north-east gives a pleasant downhill run to return to the Howard Eaton Trail junction. By going left to a water tank, before starting down one gets a good downhill run through the woods to the junction.

From the junction, return to the start by crossing the roads back to the Old Faithful area.

3. Upper Geyser Basin & Biscuit Basin YS

> **Distance:** 5 miles   **Difficulty:** Moderate
> **Time Required:** Full day   **Terrain:** Flat
> **Start elevation:** 7,360ft   **Elevation gain:** 0ft
> **Best time of year:** mid-December to mid-March

The epitome of Yellowstone ski touring. If you only have time to do one tour from the Old Faithful area, this is the one to do. The trail takes in thermal features and reasonably close encounters with wildlife. Bison, elk and coyote are all common on this trail, particularly near the various geyser areas. Remember, do not get too close!

From the Old Faithful Geyser there are several options. One is to go northwest along the trail south of the river for 1 mile to the Daisy Group. There you

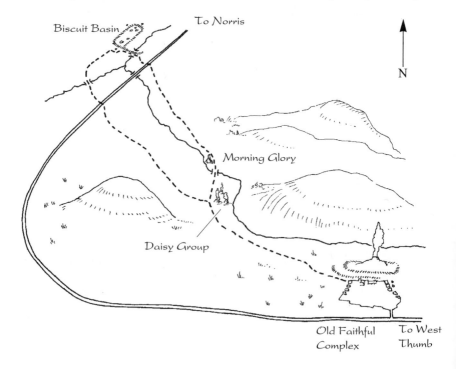

Upper Geyser Basin.

Photo: R. DuMais

can go left around Daisy, then right again following a good trail which eventually crosses the road. It then takes the footbridge over the stream and through clearings - often with little snow due to melting - to Biscuit Basin. Head east through the Basin towards the river. Cross the river using the bridge and then cross the road to a trail heading back upstream along the north-east side of the river.

After about a mile you pass the beautiful Morning Glory Pool. Cross the bridge over the river (note the Riverside Geyser which erupts frequently) and then on up the well travelled trail. Again the trail may have melted off in patches. Follow for 1¼ miles to return to Old Faithful.

Alternatively, from the Daisy Geyser Group, do the tour in the opposite direction, or one can ski out and back via either of the routes described. On the final section of the tour described, one can incorporate a loop through Geyser Hill, crossing the Firehole to get there, and back via foot bridges. This adds lots of geysers, but due to considerable foot traffic, and ice from geyser steam, it can be rather crusty and awkward.

Those seeking a longer trip can continue past the Biscuit Basin up to Mystic Falls. This adds almost a mile each way, and involves slightly harder and steeper skiing.

4. Fairy Falls

YS

Distance: 11 miles	**Difficulty:** Moderate
Time Required: Full day	**Terrain:** Flat & rolling. Good trail.
Start elevation: 7,255ft	**Elevation gain:** 100ft
Best time of year: mid-December to mid-March	

The trip to Fairy Falls is long, but worthwhile as the Falls are remote and quite pretty.

Start by taking the shuttle (small charge) from the Snow Lodge to the Fountain Flat Drive. From the drop-off, cross the bridge over the Firehole River and ski along the Fountain Flat Drive past the Grand Prismatic Spring. Just past the spring (about 1 mile out) there is a trail, well signed, going off to the left (west). Take this through lodgepole forest. It is well blazed. The trees hereabouts were burned in the 1988 fires. The trail follows the base of steep hillsides to the south as it approaches the Falls. The Falls are wildly beautiful and freeze into frozen curtains of ice that are very photogenic and one of the finest

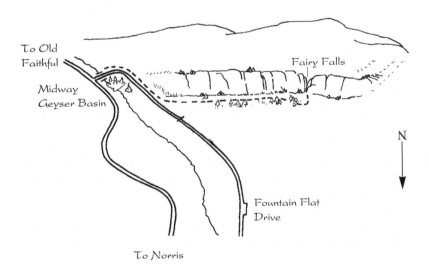

Fairy Falls in winter.

Photo: R. DuMais

winter sights the Park has to offer.

Retrace your route back to the starting point at the Fountain Flat Drive and the main loop road. Cross the road and take the trail as it goes up a short hillside into forest. For the next 3 miles the trail goes south through the trees, following a parallel course to the main road. There are many slight ups and downs until the trail reaches the Biscuit Basin.

The best route from the Basin is to stay on the left (east) side of the river and following the trail for another mile to reach the Morning Glory Pool. Cross the Firehole River using the bridge and continue on the right side of the stream using a good paved path. There may be melted patches on the path along here. It is about another 1¼ miles back to Old Faithful.

This trail is really too long to do as a complete loop, which is why using the shuttle makes it worthwhile and a reasonable trip to do at this time of year.

Skiing on Angle Mountain, Togwotee Pass. Tetons in the distance.
Photo: R. DuMais

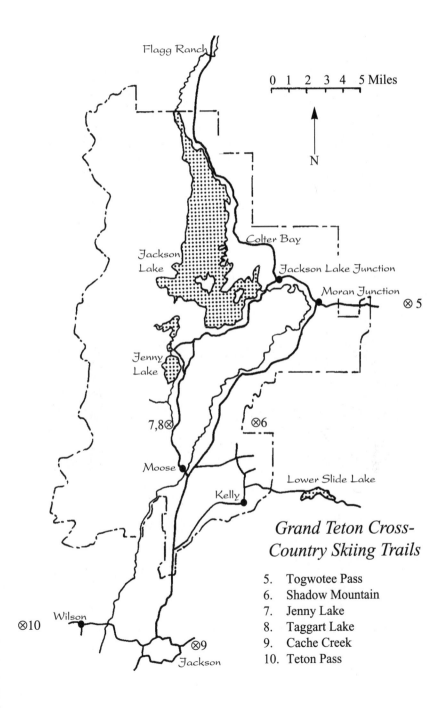

Grand Teton Cross-Country Skiing Trails

5. Togwotee Pass
6. Shadow Mountain
7. Jenny Lake
8. Taggart Lake
9. Cache Creek
10. Teton Pass

5. Togwotee Pass   `GT`

The Togwotee Pass area is high with steep and spectacular rocky peaks. Due to the high altitude of the area, it gets lots of snow and is good both early and late in the season. Note that the area is popular with snowmobilers, so care should be exercised. The backcountry around here is remote and serious. There is severe avalanche risk in places. The trails listed here will take the best part of a day to complete. Best time for skiing here is December through March.

Brooks Lake

Length: 10 miles   **Difficulty:** Moderate
Start elevation: 9,442ft   **Elevation gain:** -400ft

Start at Wind River Lake turnout. This is a small turnout ¼ mile east of the Continental Divide Parking area at the summit of Togwotee Pass, 56 miles north-east of Jackson on Hwy. 187.

From the lake, follow an old road that goes east contouring the hillside above the highway. After 3½ miles, you reach Barbers Point. Just beyond here the trail crosses some slopes that are very avalanche prone, and should only be crossed when safe snow conditions permit. In addition, the trail drops steeply down to the lake, altitude that must be regained on the return trip. For these reasons, many people ski just as far as here, take in the views, then turn back.

The return trip, via the same route, involves a 400ft climb. Alternatively, ski out on the Brooks Lake road to reach the highway after a few miles, at a point 8 miles east of the start. Hitch back or car shuttle back to the start. This way back is basically a easy ski along the road.

Angle Mountain

Length: 6 miles   **Difficulty:** Difficult
Start elevation: 8,561ft   **Elevation gain:** 1,700ft

Togwotee Lodge lies 47 miles north-east of Jackson on Highway 287. There is a Touring Center with packed trails on open rolling meadows to the north and north-east of the Lodge. The Touring Center is not as busy as the Lodge, and is a good alternative for skiers wanting to get away from the popular trails around Jackson.

Up to the north-east of the lodge is Angle Mountain's west summit. At 10,205ft Angle Mountain is a real mountain and makes a fine destination for a trip. The wide open slopes on the west end of the peak, originally cut for a proposed ski area, offer great tele/downhill skiing, although they do require a considerable climb. The summit itself has outrageous views, and although it is a

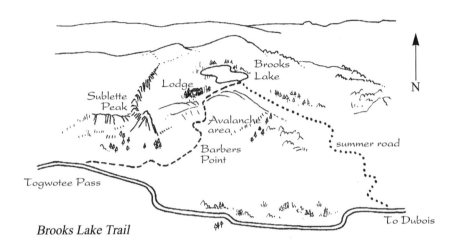

Brooks Lake Trail

Togwotee Pass.

Photo: R. DuMais

long, steep climb, it is a great outing with lots of good downhill skiing on the descent.

From the parking turnout ¼ mile east of the Lodge, go north to the base of open, west facing slopes. Climb these, staying on the south side of the peak on the final part of the ascent to reach the narrow summit ridge.

Ski back down this route. The south side of the mountain is steep, rocky with narrow gullies and should be avoided.

Blackrock Meadows

East of Togwotee Lodge are miles of rolling open meadows. There are several parking areas along the highway, and from any of these it is straightforward to head off to the south and across the meadows as far as you wish.

Descending from Angle Mountain in fine conditions.
Photo: R. DuMais

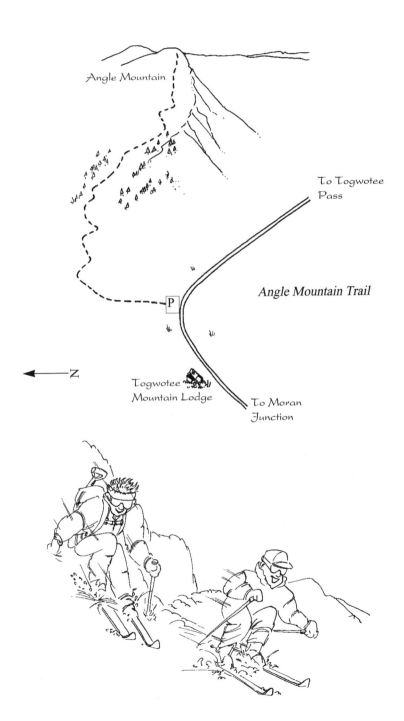

Angle Mountain

To Togwotee Pass

Angle Mountain Trail

P

← N

Togwotee Mountain Lodge

To Moran Junction

6.   Shadow Mountain   `GT`

Distance: 8 miles	**Difficulty:** Moderate
Time Required: Half day	**Terrain:** Woods & open hillsides
Start elevation: 6,723 ft	**Elevation gain:** 1529 ft
Best time of year: December - April	

An outstanding moderate tour. A gradual climb uphill, following a summer dirt road. The descent is usually packed and quite fast. Shadow Mountain is very popular with snowmobilers, particularly at weekends. Pay attention, and move aside when they pass. Along the way you have incredible views on a clear day - especially to the west, across the valley - of the entire Teton Range. Note: When parking at the trailhead be sure not to block the road as private residences further up need access.

From Jackson, go 6 miles north on the main highway to Moran Junction. Take a right (east) towards Gros Ventre and Kelly. Past Kelly the road turns north and go for 4 miles to a junction. Go straight ahead (north) to parking area,

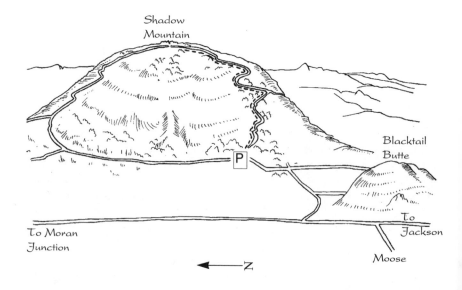

Shadow Mountain, with Grand Teton behind.

Photo: R. DuMais

just past the point where the road turns right (¾ mile from junction). Park well off the road.

Ski north-east along the dirt road for ½ mile to a marked trailhead for Shadow Mountain. Head east, following road as it climbs up through aspen woods, zigzagging as it gains height. Near the top you come out into open slopes to reach the ridgetop, some 3 miles from the start. Now head north along the ridge to the rolling open plateau at the top of Shadow Mountain (1 mile).

To descend from the summit, ski back down the route. Alternatively, slant south-west across the big open slopes below the ridge to rejoin the road further down.

7.   Jenny Lake   GT

Distance: 8 miles	Difficulty: Easy
Time Required: Full day	Terrain: Flat, wooded & open
Start elevation: 6,600ft	Elevation gain: 200ft
Best time of year: December - April	

The ski trip to Jenny Lake is one of the most scenic in the area, and a gen-uine classic. If you only have time for one trip in the vicinity, this is the one to do. If the prevailing south/south-east winds are working, then it may take twice as long to do the return section.

The trail starts at the Taggart Lake Trailhead. From Jackson head north for 10 miles on Hwy. 191/89 to the turn off for Moose. Drive across the Snake River and past the park entrance into the Park. The trailhead is 3½ miles from the Park entrance. Note that during the winter months the road is closed to vehi-cles beyond this point.

From the trailhead, follow the road north for a few hundred feet to

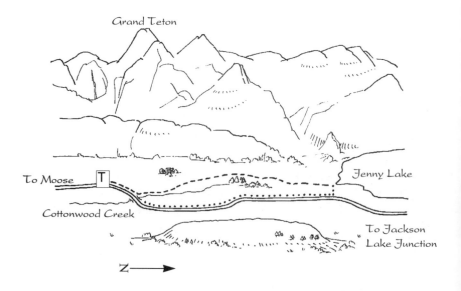

Skiing into Jenny Lake.

Cottonwood Creek. Do not cross the creek, instead turn left and head north paralleling both the creek on your right and the ever-present Teton Range on your left.

After about a mile you will see a cluster of cabins on your left. This is the Climbers Ranch, run by the American Alpine Club, and closed during the winter months. Behind the Ranch there is evidence of the 1985 fire that swept through here.

The trail continues on through sections of woods and then across the vast open Lupine Meadows to reach the shore of Jenny Lake. This is a good place for a picnic, and an opportunity to load more film into the camera.

The return journey can be a simple retrace of your route, or, strike out east for about ¼ mile to the closed road. This can then be followed back to the trailhead.

8.   Taggart Lake

`GT`

Distance: 5 miles	**Difficulty:** Moderate
Time Required: Half day	**Terrain:** Rolling & wooded
Start elevation: 6,600ft	**Elevation gain:** 300ft
Best time of year: December - April	

An ever-popular trail, in winter or summer, this is a good trip for new Cross-Country skiers looking to improve their skills. The fire that burnt many of the trees around Taggart Lake had the beneficial effect of opening up the vista so the trip is more scenic than it used to be.

The trail starts at the Taggart Lake Trailhead. From Jackson head north for 10 miles on Hwy. 191/89 to the turn off for Moose. Drive across the Snake River and past the park entrance into the Park. The trailhead is 3½ miles from the Park entrance.

From the parking lot, head west across the open area towards the line of low bluffs that parallel the road. Just before the base of the bluffs, turn right and

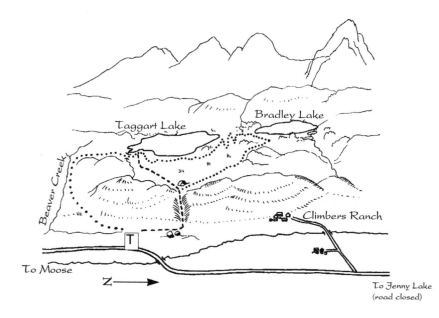

The Tetons from the Taggart Lake trail.

Photo: R. DuMais

head north. The trail follows the base of the bluffs, past some cabins before swinging around to the west into a narrow ravine and gaining height.

An open area is gained with Taggart Lake ahead. The trail branches at a large boulder. Take the left trail and head across the open area to reach the lake shore near a bridge over the outlet. From this point you have several alternatives. The first is to turn around and return the way you came in.

An alternative route back to the trailhead is via Beaver Creek. Cross the bridge and head up onto the narrow shoulder to the south. From the shoulder, continue down to the south for a short distance before following the bluff on the left around to the east. The trail follows the Beaver Creek for about a mile before you turn around to the north and head back to the meadows by the trailhead.

It is also possible to extend the tour by continuing on to Bradley Lake. This adds about another 2 miles. From the large boulder on the trail, continue straight on instead of taking the left. The trail heads up onto a shoulder that separates Taggart and Bradley Lakes. A short steep descent leads down to the shore of Bradley Lake. For the return, retrace your route onto the ridge, then instead of following a gradual descent down to the left, it is possible to head directly down to Taggart Lake across open meadows, then follow the lake shore to the outlet bridge mentioned earlier.

9.   Cache Creek

`GT`

Distance: 10 miles	**Difficulty:** Moderate
Time Required: Half day	**Terrain:** Bottom of wooded valley
Start elevation: 6,450ft	**Elevation gain:** 200ft
Best time of year: December - April	

A gradual, but steady climb just outside the town of Jackson that is very popular with the locals. Great as a close by, short trip with a good chance of seeing moose, and the occasional grouse and coyote. Due to its popularity, the snow becomes packed and this can make the descent rather fast. The trail is also popular with snowmobilers - move aside when you hear them, as visibility is not always good.

From the center of Jackson, head east on Broadway to Redmond St. Go right on Redmond to almost the base of Snow King Mountain, where you turn left on Cache Creek Drive. Go beyond the edge of town and continue to the end of the road to the parking area. Park here.

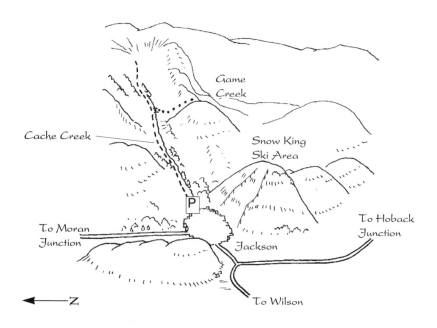

Cache Creek in winter.

Photo: R. DuMais

The route is simple and easy to follow. Ski along the snow-covered dirt road heading up the valley floor, climbing gradually.

After about 4 miles the Game Creek Trail goes off to the right. Continue on, and at the 4½ mile mark, the trail crosses a side stream from the Noker Mine Draw. Another ½ mile further up, the valley opens up considerably and branches. Beyond this point the terrain is steeper and is prone to avalanches.

The return is back the way you came in.

10. Teton Pass

Teton Pass is one of the best downhill/telemark skiing locations in the country, not only because of the terrain, but its usually superb snow and easy access. HOWEVER, this entire area, with its open slopes, steep terrain and lots of snow is very avalanche prone. Any skiing in this area should be approached with caution. In bad weather it is easy to lose your orientation. Those skiing here should be proficient at the appropriate skills (map & compass, downhill skiing, avalanche avoidance etc), carry suitable emergency gear (shovels, beepers etc) AND know how to use it. Finally, the Pass road itself can be very hazardous in bad weather.

As a good introduction, start with Ridgetop Trail, the Old Pass Road, or some of the easier, closer bowls like Telemark or Olympic. A good way to get oriented is to do the Ridgetop Trail.

To reach Teton Pass, take Hwy. 22 out of Jackson going west to Wilson. Continue west past Wilson and the road then climbs steadily to the top of the Pass. There is a large parking area on the left at the crest.

Ridgetop Trail

Length: 4 miles   **Difficulty:** Moderate
Start elevation: 8,431ft   **Elevation gain:** 769ft

Start at the west end of the parking lot. Follow the old road on the west side of the ridge for ½ mile to where it crosses the ridge crest, near power lines and Avalanche Cache. Then ski along the east side of the ridge for another ½ mile to the upper sections of Olympic Bowls. Beyond this, go up through woodland and along the flat,broad ridge crest for about a mile to open clearings above the drop to Mosquito Creek.

The way back is the same way you came in.

Old Pass Road

Length: 4 miles   **Difficulty:** Moderate - Difficult
Start elevation: 8,431ft   **Elevation loss:** -1916ft

Start from the east end of the parking lot. Head down the main highway towards Wilson for ¼ mile and the descend down to the old road below. Alternatively, ski down Telemark Bowl to reach the old road. Either way, these join and continue down main drainage. In the lower parts, it is best to stay on the old roadway which lies up on the left (north) side of the valley. This leads to the upper end of the plowed road. A car may be left here. Or go out on this past Trail Creek Ranch to reach Highway 22 near the base of the Pass. Hitch back up the Pass to your car.

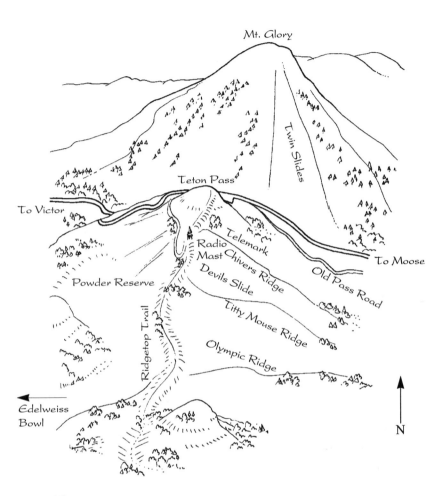

Mt. Glory

Mt. Glory is the large mountain that overlooks the top of the Teton Pass. A steep 1,500ft climb offers a number of different descents, all steep and exciting, and all only suitable for advanced skiers. The well trodden footpacked path to the summit starts across the highway from the parking lot. It takes about an hour to reach the summit.

From the Summit, to the east is Glory Bowl, a steep open avalanche chute. To the south-east is Twin Slides, another open avalanche chute to the right of the ascent line. Further round to the south are several gullies and chutes. These all end on the west side of the Pass and offer steep skiing. The farther west you go before starting down, the lower down the Pass you will come out.

To the north-west there are chutes and bowls which go down into Coal

Creek and out to a parking area at the base of the Pass, on the west side some 8 miles from the the top of the Pass.

North of Mt. Glory there is a series of steep rocky bowls on the east facing slope. These are more suited to extreme skiers and are not recommended for general use.

Other recommended routes:
South of the Pass - east facing
Telemark Bowl, probably the most popular of the bowls.
Chivers Ridge.
Devils Slide is not recommended due to avalanche risk.
Titty Mouse Ridge and Olympic Ridge.

South of the Pass - west facing
Powder Reserve.
Edelweiss Bowl, one of the best and most popular of the bowls. This is reached by taking the Ridgetop Trail to the Olympic area and then skiing down to the west, then climbing up along the left (east) edge of Edelweiss. Alternatively, take the trail to the end of the ridge going south. Then go west along the ridgeline to the top of Edelweiss.

Yurting

Yurts are a spacious Mongolian-style dwelling, about 20ft in diameter. They are usually equipped with a wood stove and can accommodate up to 8 persons. In the Tetons, a company owns and operates a small network of these huts. Offering hut tours, they will introduce you to some of the finest backcountry skiing in the region. All tours include guiding and instruction, hearty meals, sleeping gear and safety equipment.

Tours vary in length, and can be tailored for absolute beginners through to advanced skiers. Contact Rendezvous Ski Tours for more information. Their address is in the Reference Section at the back of the book.

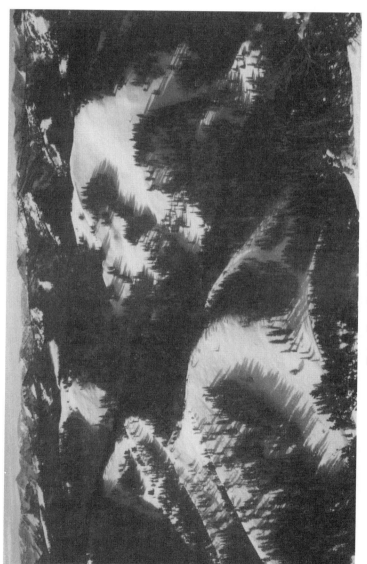

Photo: R. DuMais

Teton Pass from Mt. Glory.

Hard to tell who is having the most fun!

DOG SLEDDING

Top honors for the most romantic activity in the region must go to dog sledding. The perfect antidote to the snowmobile, the dog sled is a great way to get into the winter-bound back-country with the minimum of effort. Unless you are lucky enough to have your own team, a tour outfitter will be your only choice. Fortunately there are several to choose from.

Perhaps the biggest surprise is that the dogs are considerably smaller than they appear in the movies. The breeds you most expect to see are malamutes or samoyeds, which have been bred to be show dogs rather than working dogs. But outfitters like Frank Teasley, a six-time Iditarod competitor, prefer Alaskan Huskies as they are smart and fast. Another surprise to us was the dogs inherent good nature. The memories of fictional dog-teams with vicious traits was quickly dispelled. Even people who are not entirely happy with dogs will probably find these about as appealing as any.

When the sleds are brought out ready for a trip the dogs immediately sense an outing and a deafening cacophony of howls starts up. The dog's pleasure at going out for a run is evident to all. The same seems to be true of the tour guides who clearly have a great attachment to the dogs. No harsh words, much less whips to be found here! The key is positive reinforcement, the central premise being that the dogs are part of a team, not just the engine that pulls the sled.

As with most winter activities, ski clothing is recommended, particularly as there is not a great deal of exercise involved. The usual setup is for one passenger to lie snuggled up with a bison robe inside the sled, while the other passenger stands at the back with the guide. If you are lucky, the guide might need to take out two sleds, in which case you and another passenger may get to ride the sled without a guide. For the most part, the dogs know exactly where they are going, but the fun part is stopping them from getting too excited and overtaking the sled in front.

Tours run in various locations around the Parks, and at least one tour operator has a permit to tour inside Grand Teton National Park. It is likely however, that your tour will be in the huge National Forests that surround the Parks.

There are a variety of tours offered, including quick 1 to 2 hour tasters, through to whole-day trips with an activity such as dipping into a hot spring thrown in. The longer the tour, the more likely it will be that instead of being a passive passenger, you will actually get involved. The Jackson Hole Iditarod Sled Dog Tour Company makes a point of trying to get your involvement. This may include helping water the dogs at the end of the trip, and should include mushing the team. Most tours will include some form of refreshment stop, ranging from a snack for a half-day trip, through to a full-blown steak lunch on the whole day trip.

Before you take control of a team, you will be given a short orientation session in which you learn the basic commands, such as Gee, Haw, Whooaa, and On! (right, left, stop and go respectively). As the dogs can travel at quite a speed, a race team can achieve 0-28mph in 3 seconds on hard-packed snow, the initial 'off' is a surprise for those not familiar with the pulling power of these amazing dogs. The important thing is to hang on at all costs. The ultimate humiliation is chasing after a dog sled that has lost its musher.

A good tour guide should be able to point out features along the route, and help you spot wildlife. This is a sociable activity which can also be educational. As most of the tours will be in areas not heavily frequented by other users, the visitor will get a true wilderness experience. Many customers come back year after year. Some even request the same lead dog. You will quickly see the different personalities of the dogs, and start to understand what makes a good lead dog, and what makes a good team dog.

We can heartily recommend dog sledding to any visitor to the area. We found it to be an unexpected delight and are itching to go again!

Dog sledding on the Granite Creek Trail.

Opposite: Freddie and friend.

Fishing the Yellowstone River.

F I S H I N G

There is an amazing quantity and variety of fishing with some very high quality waters in this area. Despite these choices, the Yellowstone Lake and River and the Snake River account for perhaps 75% of all fish catches in the region. The Firehole River is perhaps one of the most unusual places to fish in the United States with geysers, hot and cold running water, a profusion of wildflowers (in season) and even bison and moose to keep you company.

Catch and release fishing methods are now practiced widely and wisely. Once you get good, better, and eventually, excellent, with your techniques we recommend removing the barbs to your hooks. A pair of nail clippers will serve as pliers for this purpose. This will improve the chances that the fish will be dehooked with minimum harm, and therefore live to provide sport another day.

As many of the waters in this area are above 6,000ft above sea level, high altitude precautions are wise. Take it easy at the start of your trip. The daytimes can be warm but night times can be chilly or even freezing. The bug season starts in June and runs through to early August.

If you want to escape the seasonal crowds, plan to visit the parks anytime after Labor Day. The latter part of September can be almost as good as August. A small amount of hiking will also help avoid the crowds, even if it is only ½ mile or so!

Fishing Licenses
Yellowstone National Park
A State Fishing License is not required in Yellowstone, but a permit is, which can be obtained at all the Entrance Stations or Visitors Centers.
Grand Teton National Park
A State Fishing License IS required in Grand Teton. These can be obtained at sporting goods stores in the state, or from the Game and Fishery Headquarters in Jackson.

1.   Blacktail Deer Creek

Length: 18 miles

Fish: Brook and cutthroat trout

Notes: An above average water

Blacktail Deer Creek (may also be known as Blacktail Creek) flows north from the Blacktail Deer Plateau to join the Yellowstone River. Access is from the Mammoth to Tower Road. There is a pullout about six miles east of Mammoth where the Blacktail Creek Trail goes north. The trail provides the easiest access to the waters close to the Yellowstone River, or else you can go off trail to find your own spot.

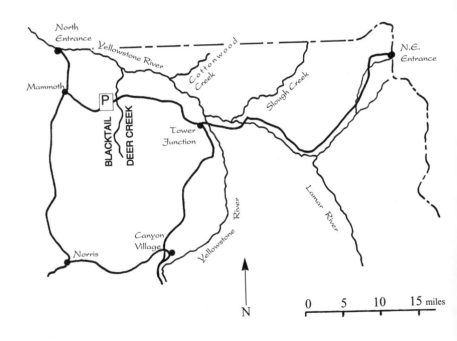

2.   Cottonwood Creek   YS

> **Length:** 3 miles
> **Fish:** Cutthroat trout
> **Notes:** Opens July 15th

The Cottonwood Creek is a tributary of the Yellowstone River, flowing in from the north. It has a well-deserved reputation as a fine cutthroat creek, albeit with small fish. A good place to get results! Cottonwood Creek reaches the Yellowstone River east of the Blacktail Creek Trail Bridge, which is situated north of the Mammoth - Tower road. The parking is the same as for Blacktail Deer Creek.

Follow the Blacktail Creek Trail north to the Yellowstone River and cross using the bridge. Then head east along the north side of the Yellowstone, crossing one small creek before reaching the Cottonwood after about 9 miles. This section takes you into the heart of the Black Canyon of the Yellowstone River and is a wild and grandiose place to spend a day.

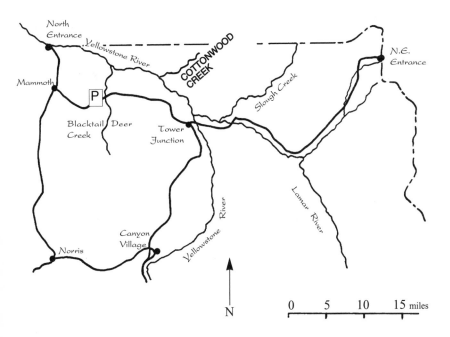

3.   Slough Creek   YS

> **Length:** 16 miles within Park, another 10 miles outside
> **Fish:** Rainbow and cutthroat trout
> **Notes:** Hiking required, except from Slough Creek Campground

Slough (pronounced 'slew') Creek flows south-west from the Gallatin National Forest into the northern section of Yellowstone Park, passing the Slough Creek Campground. It then flows into the Lamar River. Access is usually from the Campground which is reached from the Tower to North East Entrance road.

Upstream from the campground there are two distinct meadow areas after 1hr and 3hrs (2 miles and 5 miles) hiking, respectively. The waters here are for the most part gentle and peaceful in nature, giving good bank fishing.

Tip: Try the 1 hour hike via the Slough Creek Wagon Trail. You'll like the size of the fish (average 16")! Best time of year is July through Fall.

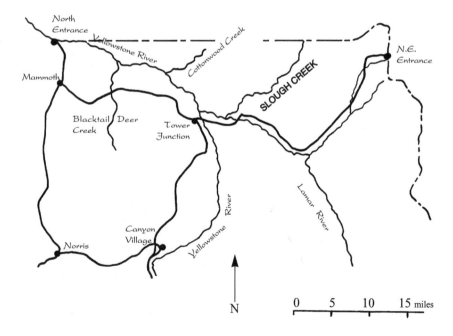

4. Lamar River

YS

> **Length:** 60+ miles
>
> **Fish:** Rainbow and cutthroat trout
>
> **Notes:** One of the longest rivers in the Park

The Lamar River starts in one of the wildest and more remote sections of the Park on its eastern edge. It flows in a northeast direction through the back-country for some 60 miles. The final 10 miles of the river, before it joins the Yellowstone River, is close to the road and consequently, receives heavy use. This is also due to its slow meadow waters.

Above the meeting with Soda Butte Creek, the Lamar runs fast through canyon country offering the challenge of catching a big one! Pocket waters also exist here.

Above the Soda Butte/Lamar junction, you must hike the Lamar River Trail. Many smaller waters flow into the Lamar. Try these as an alternative if you are not getting the results you want from the Lamar.

Best time of year is late summer.

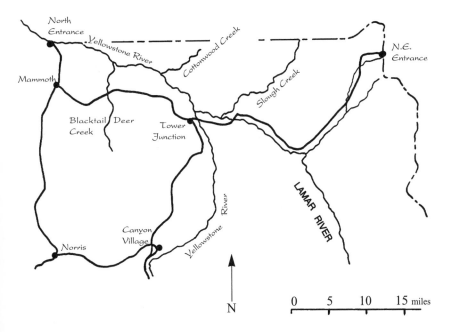

5.   Yellowstone River   `YS`

> **Length:** 70 miles within the Park
>
> **Fish:** Rainbow, brook and cutthroat trout, whitefish
>
> **Notes:** Upper section from Chittenden Bridge to Yellowstone Lake opens July 15th. Has several closed sections. See below

A big river - wet and wild - and extremely popular!

The Yellowstone river enters the park in the south-east and flows northward to the Yellowstone Lake. It then exits the lake at its northern end at Fishing Bridge before entering the Grand Canyon of the Yellowstone River. Continues north to exit the Park at Gardiner.

Best places include:

Buffalo Ford, about 5 miles north of Fishing Bridge.

A popular hike and fish trip is 7 Mile Hole, listed in the Hiking section.

Black Canyon, north west of Tower Junction.

The following sections of the Yellowstone River are closed to fishing:

1.   From its confluence with Alum Creek, upstream through the Hayden Valley to Mud Volcano. All tributary creeks into this section are also closed.

2.   From Chittenden Bridge downstream through the Grand Canyon of the Yellowstone to a point directly below Silver Cord Cascade.

3.   100 yards upstream and 100 yards downstream of LeHardy Rapids.

Best time of year is reputed to be October.

Fish Handling Tips

1. Play and land fish as quickly as possible, to avoid exhausting the catch.
2. Handle fish as little as possible and use a landing net.
3. Use wet hands. Avoid squeezing or holding the fish by the gills.
4. Keep the fish in water as much as possible.
5. Weigh fish while still in the net.
6. Remove hook gently. If hook is too deep, cut line. Hook will decompose.
7. Turn fish upside down to calm it.
8. When photographing, keep the fish in the water until the last moment.
9. When returning fish to the water, hold it in an upright position with head upstream. Move it slowly back and forth to move water through its gills. Release into calm waters.

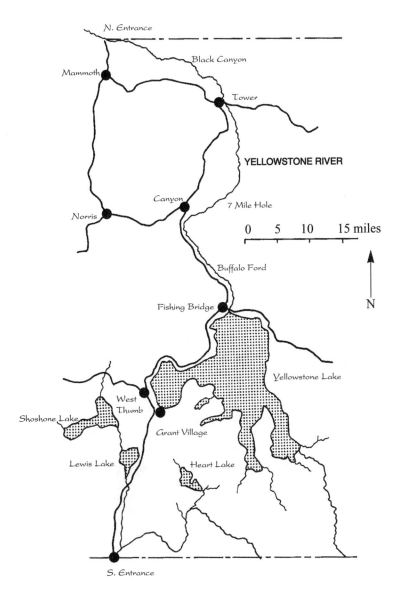

6.   Yellowstone Lake   YS

> **Size:** 136 sq. miles
>
> **Fish:** Cutthroat trout
>
> **Notes:** Certain sections of shoreline closed to fishing, see below

The Yellowstone Lake is undoubtedly a huge piece of water, North America's largest mountain lake. Located at 7,733ft above sea level, with a maximum depth of 320ft. It can, due to its size, be a potentially dangerous place in bad weather. Beware!

A sweeping statement used by some fishing aficionados states that Yellowstone Lake is the largest fishery in the world for purebred cutthroat trout!

Fishing from shore is for the most part good. Wading is also popular. Try heading out to a headland for better fishing. Boat fishing is most accessible from the northern end of the lake - Bridge Bay, Fishing Bridge, Mary Bay, West Thumb and Lake Lodge.

The cutthroat trout are greedy and go for nearly all wet flies!

Possibly the easiest place to catch fish in Yellowstone National Park.

*Note: Non-native Lake Trout were discovered in the lake recently. They pose a serious threat to the cutthroat and currently the Park is requiring fishermen to kill all lake trout caught - **only** in Yellowstone Lake - and turn them in to the Rangers. Check for up-to-date requirements.*

The following sections of Yellowstone Lake shoreline are closed to fishing:

1.   Section from West Thumb Geyser Basin to Little Thumb Creek.

2.   The section of Yellowstone River at Fishing Bridge, 1 mile upstream, ½ mile downstream.

3.   Bridge Bay Marina and Grant village marina and their connecting channels into the lake.

7.   Shoshone Lake   YS

> **Size:** 12½ sq. miles
> **Fish:** Brown and lake trout
> **Notes:** No road access

Shoshone Lake is the second largest in Yellowstone National Park and, unlike the largest, is only accessible by foot, boat or by horse. There are several backcountry campgrounds that can be utilized to make a pleasant fishing expedition. They do need to be booked in advanced at a Backcountry Office, the nearest is at Old Faithful. There is no charge to use them.

There are several access points, the nearest is from DeLacy Creek Trailhead at the north end of the lake. There is parking at the trailhead and the hike is a gentle 4 mile one through woodland. Other access points will require a longer hike. The lake can also be accessed by hand-propelled boats from Lewis Lake.

For the true backcountry fishing experience, we recommend booking one of the sites and staying over night. Sitting on the soft sand on the shoreline watching the sun go down is one of the finest Yellowstone experiences.

Best time of year is the Fall.

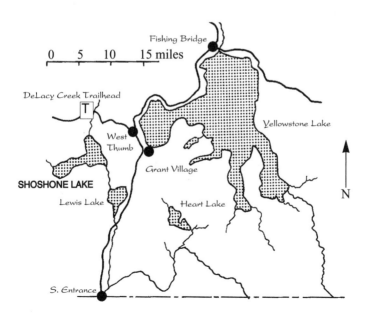

8.   Firehole River   YS

Length: 30+ miles
Fish: Brook, brown and rainbow trout, whitefish
Notes: Fly fishing only. Section near Old Faithful closed

Almost certainly the most frequented river for fly fishing in Yellowstone. The reasons for this are several. The geothermic activity close to much of this river give it an ever changing characteristic. Elk and bison often roam the region giving it a wildlife backdrop! The fish however, are wary and cunning and for this reason, the Firehole is a river that will challenge the experienced fisherman or woman. For those up to the challenge, the experience is one of the best in the region.

The river runs north from a point west of Shoshone Lake, past Old Faithful and continuing north to join the Gibbon River to form the Madison River at Madison Junction.

Note that the section where the river is to the east of the highway at Old Faithful is permanently closed to fishing.

Tips: Small flies are particularly effective on the Firehole River. Good spots are at the Biscuit Basin, large fish, and the confluence of the Little Firehole and the Firehole River.

Best time of year is early to late summer.

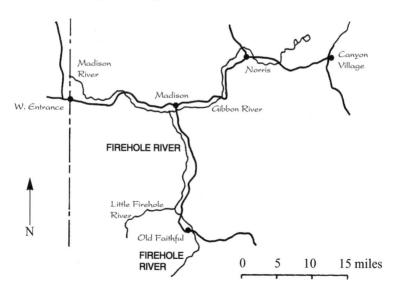

9. Gibbon River `YS`

> **Length:** 38 miles
> **Fish:** Brook, brown, rainbow and cutthroat trout, whitefish
> **Notes:** Fly fishing only from Gibbon Falls downstream

From Grebe Lake southwest to the Firehole River at Madison Junction, the Gibbon River is known for its diversity of river conditions and banks, meadows and woods. Gibbon River is a panfishery until Elk Pond.

The meadows above the falls are the most popular due to the rivers more gentle nature and the ease of wading. Below the falls the river is faster flowing. Popular spots include Gibbon Meadows and Elk Park.

Best time of year is from June through October.

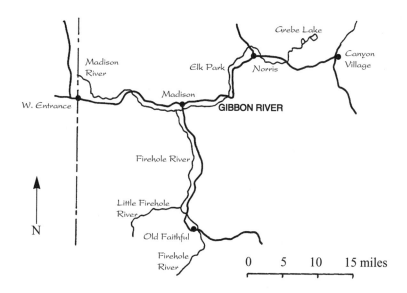

10. Madison River

> **Length:** 15 miles within Park, another 140 miles outside
> **Fish:** Brook, brown, rainbow and cutthroat trout, whitefish
> **Notes:** Fly fishing only

The Firehole River and the Gibbon River begat the Madison. The Madison, Jefferson and Gallatin begat the Great Missouri. Not surprisingly, considering the quality of the two rivers forming the Madison, it is considered by some to be the greatest fishing river in the country!

Much has been written about this very popular river, suffice to say that, given its ease of access from the road from within the Park, it probably gets the most traffic. As the hordes of fisherman and women march resolutely to the river, one can almost hear the trout whisper "Look out here they come..."

Grasshopper Bank is noted for its grasshoppers, and along with Sevenmile and Ninemile are the legendary spots on the river. Also check out the meeting of the three waters (the Firehole, Gibbon and Madison).

Best time of year is late Summer and early Fall.

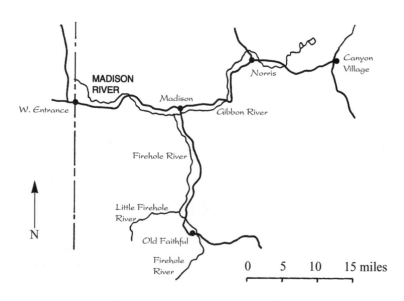

11. Gallatin River

YS

> **Length:** 30+ miles
>
> **Fish:** Rainbow, brown and cutthroat trout, whitefish
>
> **Notes:** Backcountry hiking restrictions may exist, check with Rangers

A gently flowing river, much of it is wadable. The Gallatin River flows northwest from its beginnings in the Gallatin Lake deep in the Gallatin Range. Access is usually from the road running between the West Entrance of the Park north towards Bozeman on Hwy. 191. (The upper waters can be reached by taking the Bighorn Pass Trail from Indian Creek Campground within the Park, but this is a long trip).

The fishing is above average. Most anglers choose the section near the highway although hiking into the meadows section may give better results, plus plenty of opportunity for pocket fishing. The more remote areas east of US 191 along the Bighorn Pass Trail provide more better and more challenging fishing.

Note that the Gallatin Range is prime grizzly habitat and backcountry access may be closed at certain times of the year. Check before setting out.

Tip: Try mayfly or caddis.

Best time of year is August through to late Fall.

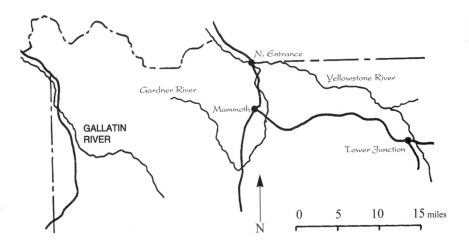

12. Gardner River

`YS`

> **Length:** 40+ miles
>
> **Fish:** Rainbow, brook, brown and cutthroat trout
>
> **Notes:** A challenging river

This river is not content to merely meander, flow or run in one general direction. Instead it begins its journey in the eastern section of the Gallatin Range near Joseph Peak. It then flows south towards Indian Creek Campground before curling round to the north to exit the Park near Gardner.

Most of the fishing on the Gardner is done on the section downstream of the Osprey Falls, or where it runs near Indian Creek Campground (although it can get crowded here).

Access from below the Osprey Falls used to be easier when the old Bunsen Peak Road was open to vehicles. Now that it is closed however, this section will need to be reached by either foot or bicycle. Lower downstream, access is possible from the Mammoth area where it is much closer to the road.

The Gardner River is open to kids, under 12, fishing with worms as bait.

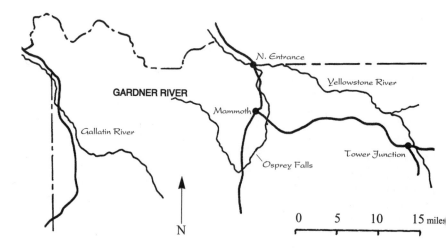

Bears and Fishermen

The national forests and national parks in the Greater Yellowstone Area are Grizzly Country. If you choose to fish and camp in this area, you need to learn about grizzly bears and how to avoid having a confrontation with one.

Grizzly bears are excellent at fishing and will often take advantage of spawning runs. In this area, they are most likely to be using the spring spawning run from May through July, although they may feed on fall spawners as well. Spawning tributaries of Yellowstone Lake within Yellowstone National Park are closed to fishing until July 15th.

Safe fishing behavior

While Fishing

Fish with a Friend. Because there is safety in numbers, avoid fishing alone. Always try to travel in pairs.

Make Noise on a Regular Basis—Especially when you are traveling through dense streamside brush. Give bears the chance to hear you coming and they will likely leave the area.

If you smell a carcass, don't investigate. Make noise, turn around or make a wide circle around it.

Learn to recognize the signs of grizzly bear activity and avoid using these areas. Typical signs of grizzly bear use near a stream include heavily used trails, fresh tracks, scat, diggings and partially eaten fish lying along the streambank.

After fishing

Gut your fish away from camping areas. Puncture the air bladder and throw the entrails into the water. Avoid getting fish odors in your clothes and wash hands thoroughly after handling fish.

Dispose of other fish remains as you would garbage. Pack it out or burn it completely. Never throw fish remains around your camp and do not bury them.

In Camp

Set up camp away from spawning streams and other water sources that may attract bears. Always keep a clean camp and follow the forest and park regulations on food storage. Avoid attracting and rewarding a bear with food.

All food and beverages; including canned food, pop and beer; garbage; grease; processed livestock or pet food; and scented or flavored toiletries (toothpaste) are bear attractants and must be stored unavailable to bears at night and when unattended during the day.

Encounters

Be prepared! Read the section on Bears on page 59.

Information courtesy of the Wyoming Game and Fish Department.

13. Snake River   `GT`

Length: 27 miles within the Park, with total length of 1,000 miles
Fish: Cutthroat trout, some brown and lake trout, and whitefish
Notes: Closed to trout fishing Nov. 1 through March 31

One of the most popular rivers in the USA, the cutthroat trout fishing is said to be very good with lengths up to 20". The Snake is felt by many to be over-fished, and can be busy during the summer months. Despite this, it is still a fine outing, never dull, with a magnificent backdrop of the mountains.

The Snake is home to a separate species of cutthroat - the Snake River Cutthroat. It differs from the normal cutthroat by the presence of hundreds of black spots on the body.

Probably the best way to fish the Snake is to float down it. The under-growth can be thick on the banks. However, it is a serious stretch of river for the boatman and the Park Service recommends only experienced boatmen try float-ing it. For more details on floating the Snake, see the Rafting Section. If you do not have a boat or lack the experience then there are numerous trips available locally however with experienced guides. Another good reason for hiring a guide is that they will be knowledgeable about recent changes in the river flow, as well as the best places to try.

All is not well on the Snake however. Due to its enormous popularity, the Snake is becoming overfished. Even regulations limiting fishing to catch and release between 11" and 18" in length has not done enough to halt the decline. Nonetheless, this is still a marvellous trip and with the help of an experienced guide, will be a trip to remember for many years afterwards. Note that fishing is restricted to artificial flies or lures only.

A good place for both the beginner and more experienced fly fisherman to experience wild native trout fishing.

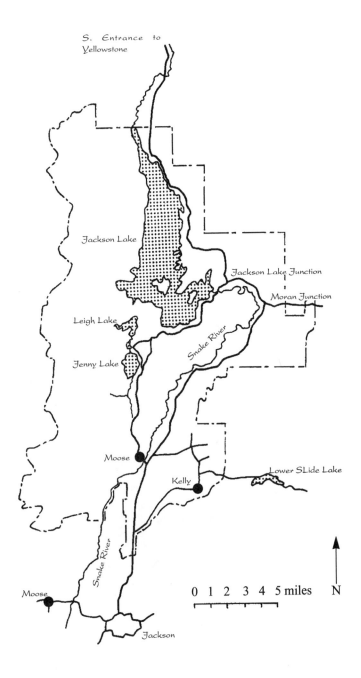

S. Entrance to Yellowstone

Jackson Lake

Jackson Lake Junction

Moran Junction

Leigh Lake

Snake River

Jenny Lake

Moose

Kelly

Lower SLide Lake

Snake River

Moose

0 1 2 3 4 5 miles   N

Jackson

14. Jackson Lake

GT

> **Size:** 31 sq. miles
>
> **Fish:** Lake trout (mackinaw), cutthroat, brook and brown trout
>
> **Notes:** Closed to fishing October 1 through October 31

Jackson Lake offers good fishing with excellent sized lake trout up to 40lb. During the height of summer most of the fish will have gone deep, but early on after the ice has broken up the fishing from shore can be good.

Elevation is 6,772ft. Maximum depth is 425ft.

Campgrounds at Signal Mountain, Colter Bay, Lizard Creek as well as the Jackson Lake Lodge.

Ice fishing on Jackson Lake in January.
Note the snowplane, a common sight on the lake in winter.

15. Jenny Lake GT

> **Size:** 2 sq. miles
>
> **Fish:** Lake, brown, brook and cutthroat trout, whitefish
>
> **Notes:** Motor-powered boats in excess of 7.5hp prohibited

A gem in the heart of the Tetons. 30-40lb'ers have been pulled from Jenny Lake. shore fishing is at its best during the summer months. Springtime can be a pleasant surprise when the ice starts to melt in the inlets and outlets. It is also a more peaceful place at that time of year.

During the height of the summer the fish in the lake are probably outnumbered by the tourists around its edge.

Best time of year is June and July.

A float trip on the Snake River.

16. Lower Slide Lake

GT

> **Size:** 1 sq. mile
>
> **Fish:** Cutthroat, lake and rainbow trout
>
> **Notes:** Interesting area for the rest of the family!

Less visited than the other more popular lakes in Grand Teton Park, it can provide solitude. The Gros Ventre River is also worth a look, again uncrowded. The lake was formed by the blocking of the Gros Ventre River as a result of the Gros Ventre Slide in 1925.

Boat launching is available at the Atherton Creek Campground. No rentals are available.

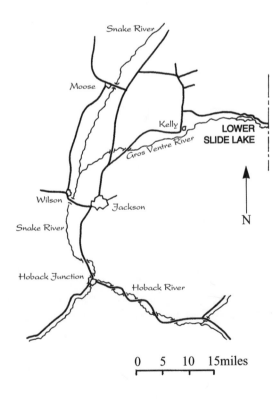

17. Gros Ventre River `GT`

> **Length:** 80 miles
> **Fish:** Cutthroat trout and whitefish
> **Notes:** Closed to fishing November 1 through May 20

The river makes for an excellent alternative to the popular Snake. Considered a poor river for floating, it nevertheless is a greater 'wilderness' alternative and the scenery is a refreshing change from the usual Teton views.

The Gros Ventre River flows in a generally easterly direction though the Lower Slide Lake to join the Snake River 5 miles north of Wilson.

Often shallow and wide, it contains plenty of interest for the angler with riffles and pocket water. Irrigation may effect the water level, so check locally before setting out. There are also some special regulations which should be checked at the same time.

Once a 'trade route' in the days when trappers roamed the hills for beaver, the Gros Ventre Valley saw much of the traffic coming into the area. Nowadays it is a peaceful, scenic region.

Best time of year is July and August.

18. Hoback River `GT`

> **Length:** 43 miles
> **Fish:** Cutthroat trout and whitefish
> **Notes:** Scenic and close to the highway

The Hoback River, a tributary of the Snake, is at first glance very appealing. Originating in the Upper Bridger Teton region, it flows south toward Hoback Junction. Sadly the fishing is not world class. It is however, still worthwhile, and the scenery and quiet makes it a good location. The river is fishable for about 10 miles along Highway 187 east from Hoback Junction, and there are sections of private land to avoid. It is a fast-flowing river and the waters can be murky after rain and during the spring run-off.

The best section is reputed to be 5 miles east and upstream of Hoback Junction.

Another day at the office!
Photo: Grand Valley Aviation

FLYING & GLIDING

Home of the 'Super Teton Ride', gliding gives a unique viewpoint on the Tetons. It's an exciting one hour glider flight around the Grand Teton, reaching an altitude of 12,000ft, and is billed as the Ultimate Glider Ride in the West. Other, shorter riders are also available. The shortest ride, of about 15 minutes, ascends 2,000ft above the Teton Valley before gently descending back to the airfield. A 30 minute ride takes you higher and circles the Grand Targhee Resort. In the glider there is only room for one passenger at a time, but due to the oversize canopy, you do get a marvellous view. If you have the time, a license to be able to fly a glider in the presence of a fully licensed pilot takes about two days, while a full solo license will take about a week to complete.

Also available are flights in 4-seater, single engine Cessna 182's. At least two companies offer flights over the region. These can be standard scenic flights or custom tours. Three passengers can be carried, and with a full plane load, the price becomes very reasonable.

From the Driggs airfield in Idaho, and the Jackson Hole Airport, two companies offer similar scenic flights. A one hour flight will take in both sides of the Tetons, as well as southern Yellowstone, while a 1½ to 2 hour flight will cover Yellowstone as well.

There is also a company operating scenic flights out of Yellowstone Regional Airport in Cody, and they also offer charter flights.

Flights are offered throughout the day and all year round, weather permitting. They do however need to be booked in advance, we have listed the companies and their phone numbers in the references at the back of the book.

Perfecting that swing!

G O L F

If it was just the scenery that made playing golf in this area a unique experience, then that would be enough reason alone to bring your clubs. There is however, more than just a pretty backdrop to play against. The courses in this area rank amongst the finest in the country, and where else can you have the possibility of having bison or elk play through?

Legend has it that golf balls fly further this high above sea level. We were sure that this was mere wishful thinking, but Jeff Heilbrun, Resort Manager at Teton Pines, assures us that golf balls do indeed travel about 10% further at this altitude.

The golfing season is fairly short, reflecting the length of the long, harsh winter. Most courses will be open May through October, but this may change according to the conditions. In part due to this short season, the Teton Pines Resort offers other activities as well, and is open throughout the year.

1. Jackson Hole Golf and Tennis Club

Holes: 18
Open to Public: Yes   **Cost for 18 holes:** $72
Carts available: Yes   **Telephone:** (307) 733-3111

Comments: A Par 72 course designed by Bob Baldock and redesigned by Robert Trent Jones Jr. A fairly flat course with uninterupted views of the Tetons. Green fee includes the use of a golf cart and range balls. Putting greens and driving range. Other facilities include tennis courts, restaurant, snack bar, lounge and changing rooms. Lessons are available, call for details.
Has been rated by Golf Digest amongst the top ten public courses in the US.

2. Teton Pines

Holes: 18
Open to Public: Yes   **Cost for 18 holes:** $70-$95
Carts available: Yes - included   **Telephone:** (307) 733-1005

Comments: Course designed by Arnold Palmer and Ed Seay. Putting greens and driving range. The course has been designed with 42 acres of lakes, created more for aesthetic reasons than as obstacles. Four different sets of tees for all levels of ability. Other facilities include tennis courts, restaurant, lounge and changing rooms. There is also an award-winning golf shop. Teton Pines is open year round, offering tennis and cross-country skiing during the winter.
Note: Teton Pines has a dress code, ie. collared shirts for gentlemen.

3. Targhee Village Golf Course

Holes: 9
Open to Public: Yes   **Cost for 9 holes:** $7
Carts available: Yes - $7   **Telephone:** (208) 354-8577

Comments: Course designed by Bud Munson. A very open course, that is fairly easy to play. Driving range. Other facilities include pro shop and snack counter.
Located in the foothills west of the Tetons, just outside the town of Alta.

A driving range with a marvellous view. Jackson Hole Golf and Tennis Club.

The Lower Falls of the Yellowstone River.

H I K I N G

Hiking must be the best way to see the Yellowstone and Grand Teton National Parks. In exchange for the expenditure of a small amount of energy and effort, the hiker is rewarded with sights and sounds that could never be seen from an automobile, to say nothing of the peace and quiet. It is quite amazing how short a distance one has to travel from the road to avoid the crowds. Obviously, some trails are so popular they will be busy during the height of the summer. The trail around Jenny Lake to Hidden Falls in Grand Teton must rank as one of the busiest in any National Park. Other trails however, and we have tried to identify some of them in this chapter, will amply reward the solitude seeking hiker.

When setting out on one of these trails, there are, as usual, a few items that the wise hiker will carry with them. Perhaps the biggest threat to the hiker is the weather. At the altitude of this area, storms can roll through at any time bringing rain or snow and turn a fine summers day into an unpleasant battle with the elements. Therefore, some sort of rain gear is essential. Choice of footwear is as much a personal choice as anything else. Ankle support is always a practical idea as many trails are rough and can easily turn an ankle. Good solid boots are recommended for the mountain trails. A map and compass are always a good idea for the longer hikes.

The 'Hello' Factor

It is our experience that when hikers meet other hikers on the trail, there seems to be some confusion as to whether they should greet each other. After extensive research we believe we have the definitive rule. Greeting is to take place when you have travelled in excess of 3 miles from the trailhead. The choice of salutation is left to the conscience of the individual hiker, although the shorter the better is generally the accepted rule. If you commit the ultimate sin of greeting closer to the trailhead, and elicit no response, do not despair! Console yourself with suitable gestures about 100 yards further on.

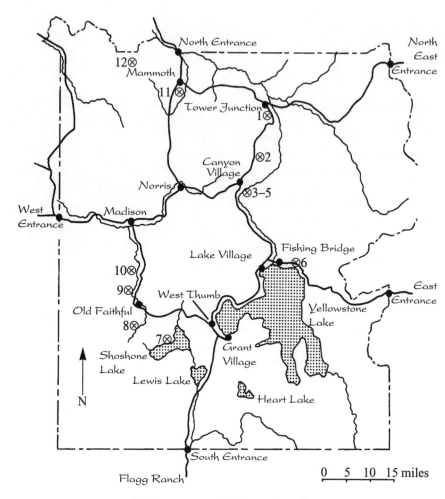

Yellowstone Hiking Trails

1. Tower Falls
2. Mt. Washburn
3. Uncle Tom's
4. North Rim Trail
5. 7 Mile Hole
6. Storm Point
7. Shoshone Lake
8. Lone Star Geyser
9. Mystic Falls
10. Fairy Falls & Imperial Geyser
11. Bunsen Peak
12. Electric Peak

1. Tower Falls

YS

Distance: 2½miles	**Difficulty:** Easy
Time Required: 1 hr	**Terrain:** Good, metaled trail
Start elevation: 6,510ft	**Elevation loss:** 220ft
Best time of year: Summer	

Tower Falls is another popular honey pot for the car-bound sightseer.

Despite this, it is a pleasant short walk.

Park at the Tower Falls parking lot. The trail, which is metaled, leads to an overlook of the falls. Some may feel that is enough, but greater reward awaits those who descend down to near the base of the falls. The rock walls loom menacingly overhead and provides a grand setting for what is otherwise a fairly unremarkable waterfall.

2.   Mt. Washburn

YS

> **Distance:** 6½ miles   **Difficulty:** Moderate
> **Time Required:** 3 hrs   **Terrain:** Disused road
> **Start elevation:** 8,840ft   **Elevation gain:** 1,400ft
> **Best time of year:** Summer

Mt. Washburn must rank as one of the most popular short hikes in the park, and deservedly so. It offers a fine walk, coupled with a commanding view of the park as well as a good chance of seeing bighorn sheep. A good time for the hike is early evening when there will be fewer people around and the evening sun will be less severe on your back.

The peak can be climbed from either the south, from Dunraven Pass Parking Area, or from the north, from the Chittenden Parking Area. there isn't much to choose between them, although the northern approach is open to bicycles so this may, or may not, sway your decision.

Neither trail is hard to find or follow as they use disused roads to the sum-

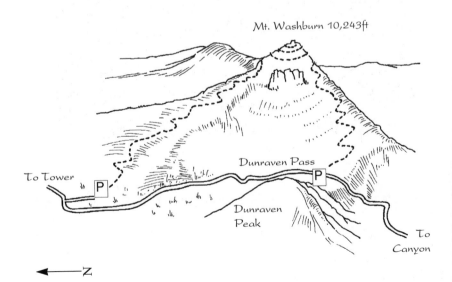

Mt. Washburn 10,243ft

To Tower

Dunraven Pass

Dunraven
Peak

To
Canyon

N

Yellowstone Lake from Mt. Washburn summit.

mit, joining up near the top where the final section corkscrews around to reach the prominent Fire Watch station that adorns the summit.

There is a room open to the public on the ground floor of the tower with big windows looking east and south. From here you can watch others making their way up and gloat that you have already made it, and also perhaps wonder why the Park Service felt it was really necessary to provide such facilities.

3.   Uncle Tom's   `YS`

> **Distance:** 1 mile   **Difficulty:** Easy
> **Time Required:** 1 hr   **Terrain:**   Good trail and steep stairs
> **Start elevation:** 7760ft   **Elevation loss:** 500ft
> **Best time of year:** Summer to early Fall

Uncle Tom's trail is an exciting short trip down into the canyon to get a view of the Lower Falls from a face on angle.

The trail starts from the Uncle Tom's parking area on the Artist Point Road on the south side of the canyon. Initially a metaled path, the trail soon descends steeply down into the canyon using metal steps - some 300 of them. The steps are steep and can be quite intimidating for those unhappy with heights. There are good handrails to grip onto though, and the view of the falls is worth the effort. Effort is a good word for the ascent back up, but console yourself with the thought that in the old days, Uncle Tom used all sorts of ropes and ladders for this trip!

Pikas.

Descending Uncle Tom's.

4. North Rim Trail

Distance: 6 miles	**Difficulty:** Easy
Time Required: 3 - 4 hrs	**Terrain:** Mainly level, good trail
Start elevation: 7780ft	**Elevation gain:** 0ft
Best time of year: Summer to early Fall	

The North Rim trail allows you to see much of the Canyon while, for the most part, avoiding the crowds.

The trail starts from the Chittenden Bridge over the Yellowstone River, just south of the Upper Falls. There is a metal gate here. Walk past this and follow the metaled road over another bridge (interesting islands in the river to your right here) and on to the Brink of the Falls trail which leads down to the top of the Upper Falls. The North Rim trail continues on through the parking lot to a point just up the road where it breaks away and soon gives a view of the Crystal Falls, a delicate falls, in contrast to the main Falls. As you head further east, the trail becomes progressively less maintained, but never too difficult. The next junction is with the short trail to the Brink of The Lower Falls. This is a more spectacular viewpoint the the brink of the Upper Falls and recommended. It also gives a fine view of Uncle Tom's trail opposite.

Once back on the rim again, the trail ambles on to Lookout Point and then to Inspiration Point. Inspiration Point - a very popular viewpoint - is the place to get a good long shot of the Lower Falls in the distance. The best part about hiking this section of the trail is the relative solitude, broken only by the crowds at the two 'points'.

While on the trail, keep an eye out for osprey that nest on rock spires in the canyon and fish in the river.

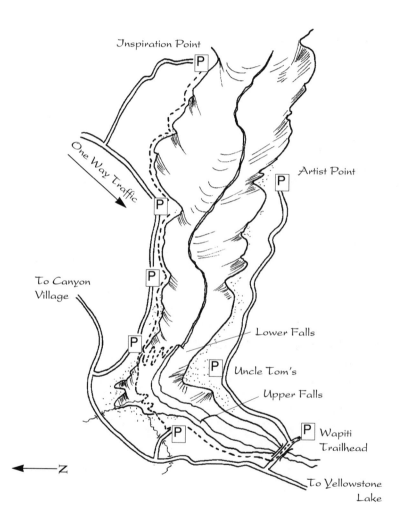

The Upper Falls of the Yellowstone River.

The Grand Canyon of the Yellowstone River.

5.   7 Mile Hole

`YS`

> **Distance:** 10 miles   **Difficulty:** Difficult
> **Time Required:** 6 hrs   **Terrain:**   Steep, in places loose, trail
> **Start elevation:** 7,840ft   **Elevation loss:** 1,080ft
> **Best time of year:** Summer to early Fall

7 Mile Hole, so called because it is seven miles downstream from the Lower Falls, is a fine trip down into the Canyon. A strenuous climb out of the Canyon may not suit the unfit, particularly as some of it is exposed to the full force of the summer sun. Warning - take plenty of water as potable water is not available in the Canyon.

Park at the Glacial Boulder parking area on the Inspiration Point road. The trail heads north east along the rim of the canyon, past the Silver Cord Cascade Overlook. The woodland you walk through was not burnt in the 1988 fires, and seems to support a multitude of irritating mosquitoes! This initial part of the trip is fairly level. After about 2 miles a short descent, with a brief glimpse of

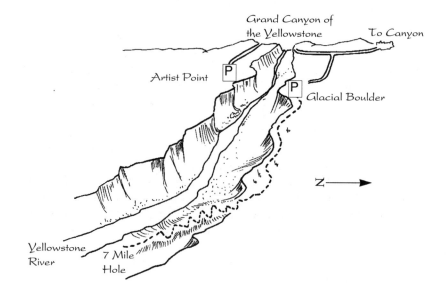

7 Mile Hole and the Yellowstone River.

Mt. Washburn and its distinctive Fire Tower, lead to a lush meadow area. This is past on the right and soon after you start the descent into the canyon. Predictably the trail gets steeper here. A fumarole with a fine cone is passed and elk are can often be seen around here. As you get lower you come out of the trees and into a larger geothermic area. The path can be quite steep here and the footing loose. A junction is then reached in the trail with cryptic signs - to the right is "4C1", to the left is "4C2,3,4". These do in fact refer to backcountry campsites - they need to be booked before setting out at the Park Rangers Station - which can make a nice overnight trip out of this hike.

7 Mile Hole is to the left here. The trail goes back into the trees for some welcome relief from the sun, before a short steep descent leads down to the junction of Sulphur Creek and the Yellowstone River. Sulphur Creek is well named as it has a cloudy, unattractive look about it. This is 7 Mile Hole and a good spot for lunch.

The return trip can be hot and dusty as you climb out of the Canyon - you will need that extra water to drink!

6. Storm Point

YS

Distance: 2 miles   **Difficulty:** Easy
Time Required: 1hr.   **Terrain:** Largely level trail
Start elevation: 7,780ft   **Elevation gain:** 0ft
Best time of year: Summer to early Fall

Note: Storm Point Trail is in prime grizzly habitat and is often closed as a result. It may be safest to check at the Ranger Station at Bridge Bay before setting out.

The hike out to Storm Point is probably on of the best short walks in the Yellowstone National Park. Storm Point juts out into Yellowstone Lake and gives a fine viewpoint of the lake as well as the peaks to the south and east.

Park at the Indian Pond (previously called Squaw Lake) trailhead and hike out towards the lake following the trail. Indian Pond was created by a hydrothermal explosion which left behind the distinctive crater.

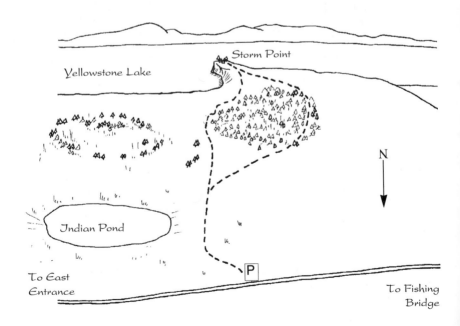

Diamond Beach, as seen from Storm Point

Sometimes bear scat (droppings) can be seen on the trail here. If it appears fresh you might want to turn around and come back another day.

Indian Lake is passed and then the trail reaches the shore of Yellowstone Lake. It turns right (west) and heads into the trees. Follow the trail through thick woodland, keeping a watchful eye out for bison and bears. The windfall is particularly thick here, in marked contrast to areas burned in recent years. After a short while you emerge from the woodland to an open area before the promontory that is Storm Point.

There are two options for the return trip. You can either retrace your steps, or make the trail into a loop. The loop trail leaves Storm Point and follows the shore of the lake west for a short distance before heading back into the forest and eventually returning to meet the main trail near Indian Pond.

7.   Shoshone Lake   YS

Distance: 20 miles   **Difficulty:** Moderate
Time Required: 2 days   **Terrain:** Good, well maintained trail
Start elevation: 8,015ft   **Elevation gain:** 200ft
Best time of year: Summer and early Fall

The hike up to Shoshone Lake is often considered one of the finest in the Park. It can be done in a day, but such is the beauty of this area, and the lake itself, that we recommend booking one of the backcountry campsites on the lake shore and staying overnight. Also this way you get to spend more time exploring the Shoshone Geyser Basin.

Remember to book a backcountry campsite before leaving. The best place to do this is the Backcountry Office at Old Faithful.

Start from the DeLacy Creek Trailhead, 9 miles south of Old Faithful on the road to West Thumb. The hike to the lake shore along DeLacy Creek is gentle and offers good opportunity for viewing elk in the river plain. As you

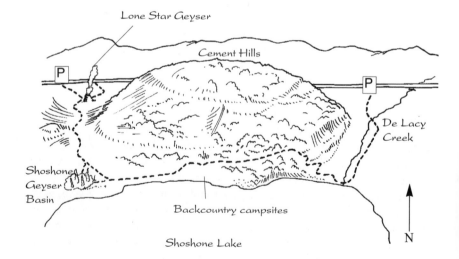

Shoshone Geyser Basin.

approach the lake the creek appears wide and suggests a wet crossing. However, it can be crossed more easily by following the trail all the way to the lake shore, then turning right (west) and following the lake shore. The inlet is only a trickle by the shore.

The trail soon heads back into the trees and then follows a winding path with glimpses of the lake to the backcountry campsites.

The next morning, continue heading west through the trees for about another 3 miles before coming to the Shoshone Geyser Basin. Unlike the geyser basins near the highway, this one lacks the built walkways and therefore considerable care must be taken exploring this area. Some years ago a hiker died after falling through the thin crust here into a very hot spring. One of the notable features here is Union Geyser with its three cones. You may be lucky to see it erupt, but as it is unpredictable, don't bet on it!

The usual way back is to retrace your steps to where you entered the geyser basin, then take the trail out to Lone Star Geyser. Just before reaching it, a junction is reached where you can decide whether to take the Howard Eaton Trail back to Old Faithful, or return by the easier route of the Lone Star Geyser road.

Either way, you will need to hitch back to your vehicle at the DeLacy Creek Trailhead.

8.   Lone Star Geyser   `YS`

Distance: 5 miles   **Difficulty:** Easy
Time Required: 3 hrs   **Terrain:** Disused road
Start elevation: 7,583 ft **Elevation gain:** 55 ft
Best time of year: Summer and early Fall

Lone Star Geyser is a fine little geyser with a prominent high cone and a regular erupting pattern of currently (1994) about 3 hours. The hike to it is straightforward and picturesque, making this is a great early evening hike with a good chance of seeing wildlife.

Park at a lot just south of the Kepler Cascades parking lot. The trail is really just a disused road (now open to cyclists as well) and is therefore easy to follow. It follows for the most part the Firehole River with lush vegetation providing prime habitat for moose, and somewhat less welcome, mosquitoes. The river is also popular with fishermen.

Once the unmistakable cone of Lone Star Geyser, so called due to it being

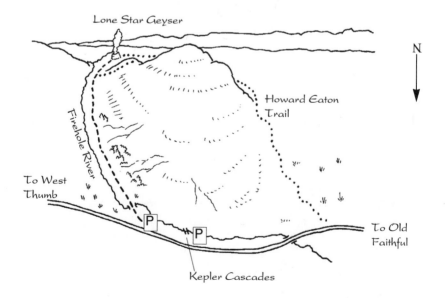

Lone Star Geyser in action.

several miles from Old Faithful, is reached, look for a notebook inside a small box on a stand. If recent visitors have made entries, it will hopefully give a clue as to the time of the next eruption. It is possible to ask at the Park Station at Old Faithful when the next eruption is due, but they do not always have that information. Anyway, if you have time, settle down and wait for Lone Star to strut it's stuff. A good book might help the time fly by. If you witness an eruption, the Park Service request that you enter the time and details into the notebook.

The return is back the way you came in.

9.   Mystic Falls

`YS`

Distance: 3½miles	**Difficulty:** Easy
Time Required: 2 hrs	**Terrain:** Good, well maintained trail
Start elevation: 7,285ft	**Elevation gain:** 460ft
Best time of year: Summer and early Fall	

The hike to Mystic Falls makes a good extension to the normal walk around the geysers at Biscuit Basin. Bison and elk are often seen in the woodland near the falls, and the viewpoint near the end of the hike provides an unusual aerial view of the basin and Old Faithful in the distance.

Start from the Biscuit Basin parking lot. Follow the boardwalk around the springs at Biscuit Basin (either direction) to the Avoca Spring where a trail heads off the boardwalk and into the trees. Shortly after, a trail register is reached. The trail follows a path through the woodland to a junction. Take the left and follow this past a trail heading off to the left to Summit Lake. Mystic Falls is soon seen in the distance and the trail approaches almost to the base.

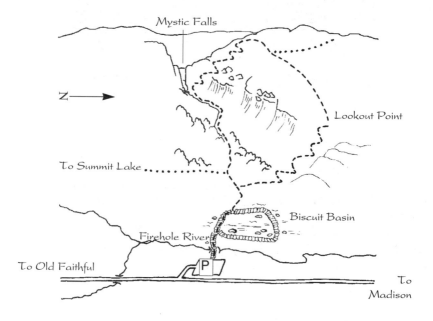

Freddie surveys Mystic Falls.

There are a number of hot springs feeding into the river here. The trail climbs up the hillside to an overlook above the falls, then zig-zags on up the hillside to a junction with another trail on the crest of a ridge. The left turn can take you to Little Firehole Meadows and Fountain Flat Drive, but we will go right to another overlook giving a good view of the Biscuit Basin, Black Sands and Old Faithful areas.

From the overlook, the final part of the trail goes down the hillside to the right through a series of zig-zags to complete the loop at the first junction. Head back to the Biscuit Basin along the way you came in.

10. Fairy Falls & Imperial Geyser   `YS`

Distance: 6 miles   **Difficulty:** Easy

Time Required: 3 hrs   **Terrain:** Good, well maintained trail

Start elevation: 7,190ft   **Elevation gain:** 100 ft

Best time of year: Summer and early Fall

Yet another trail taking in a Yellowstone waterfall. Despite this however, it is still worth doing as it also includes some interesting geothermal features which can be seen without the inevitable crowds that characterize the best known spots (the waterfall is pretty good as well!).

The trail begins from the end of the Fountain Flats Drive, just north of the Midway Geyser Basin. Follow Fountain Flat Drive to where gates stop any further progress by car. Park here. Initially the trail continues on the Drive past the gate and on towards the Midway Geyser Basin which can be seen spewing steam in the distance. Just before reaching level with the geyser basin, a trail heads off the Drive to the right (west). Hike past the trail register and on into

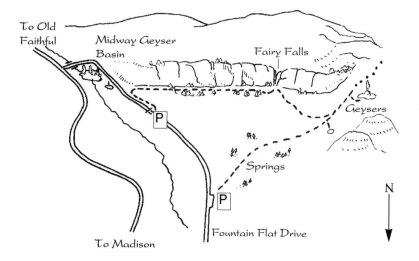

Fairy Falls

burnt woodland. For once, the telegraph poles that go through here look strangely in keeping with the woodland as they too were burnt. The trail heads steadily west on a level path following the line of bluffs to the south. After about 1½ miles the falls are reached. Once you have had your fill, continue on in the same direction, following a less well-used trail. After crossing a small meadow area, a junction and signs are reached. To the right is the return trail to Fountain Flats Drive, and to the left is a short detour to see the geyser and hot spring. Go left and soon after a side trail goes up to the small, but active, Spray Geyser. Returning to the path again continue in the direction of Imperial Geyser which is signed about a ½ mile further on.

Imperial Geyser is a wide pool with colorful algae growth and some subsidiary vents making walking around the geyser somewhat hazardous. Return to the junction at the meadow and take the trail signed for Fountain Flats Drive. After a steady level walk an area of hot springs is reached with some interesting pools. This area is obviously popular with elk as much evidence can be seen of their presence, if not the elk themselves.

Once the trail arrives back at the Drive, turn right and hike the final mile back to your car.

11. Bunsen Peak

YS

Distance: 7 miles	**Difficulty:** Moderate
Time Required: 3 hrs	**Terrain:** Steep but good trail
Start elevation: 7,150 ft	**Elevation gain:** 1,320ft
Best time of year: Summer and early Fall	

Bunsen Peak is a popular destination just outside the town of Mammoth. This trail takes you to the top of the peak, then down the other side for a spell of solitude, then back along the Bunsen Peak Road (and a detour to the Falls if you feel up to it).

Park at a small parking lot just past the Rustic Falls lot at the top of the Golden Gate Pass. Hike past the gate on the old Bunsen Peak Road, then strike up the hillside following a narrow trail. A trail register is soon reached. The trail continues in an easterly direction as it traverses the hillside above Rustic Falls. The trail zig-zags through woodland quite a lot until a meadow area is reached on a western slope. A fallen tree here provides a good resting spot as well as a great view west towards the Gallatin Mountain Range as well as the striking red

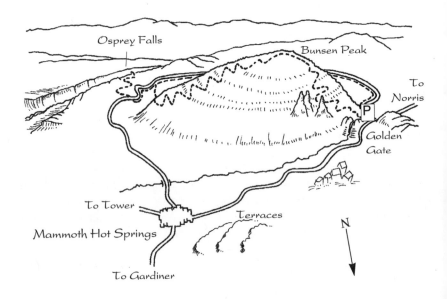

Looking towards Mammoth from part way up Bunsen Peak.

outline of Electric Peak to the north. Having caught your breath, continue up the trail. As the trail zig-zags again there is opportunity to get a view of the Terraces at Mammoth.

The final section to the top crosses some talus but the trail is never difficult. The first summit is the main summit and you may not feel inclined to tarry long by this mish-mash of aerials and a small scruffy building. Continue on a short distance to a second summit which is less heavily adorned.

From here, most turn around and head back the way they came. A more exciting option however is to follow the faint path past the third summit and down the east face of Bunsen Peak. Adventurous not for it's difficulty, rather the trail is faint and care must be taken to stay on track. You stand a good chance of seeing elk here and possibly coyote. Don't worry if the trail wanders around quite a bit, it will eventually lead down to the old road. From there turn right and follow it back to your car.

Alternatively, turn left and after a short way down the road, a trail goes back up a canyon following the Gardner River to the Osprey Falls. This detour will add about 3 miles to your trip but is worth the extra effort.

12. Electric Peak

`YS`

Distance: 20 miles   **Difficulty:** Difficult and strenuous

Time Required: 2 days   **Terrain:** Steep and loose in places

Start elevation: 7,150ft   **Elevation gain:** 3,842ft

Best time of year: Summer

Seen from Bunsen Peak, Electric Peak has an almost unreal, ethereal quality about it. Seen in the early morning, it can look blood red - very sinister. It does, however, provide an interesting ascent, best spread over two days.

You will need to book a backcountry campsite before setting out. The best sites are at the Gardner River, near the junction with the spur trail that heads up the southeast ridge of the peak. There are other sites available, only further away.

Day one starts from the Glen Creek trailhead at the Golden Gate Pass just outside Mammoth. Follow the trail north skirting the Gardner River plain, watch for bison and pronghorn, and then up a narrow ravine to reach a meadow.

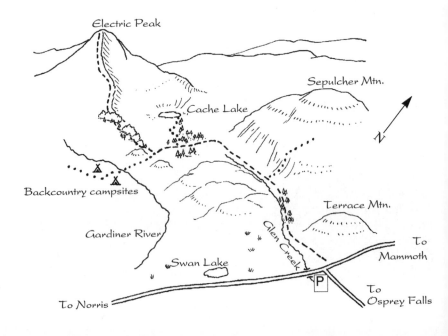

The trail follows the meadow on its righthand edge before curving around to the north then west to enter thick woodland. It can be quite a relief to get into the shade on a hot summers day! After about 1½ miles in the woods, the junction with the trail that leads up Electric Peak is reached on a shoulder. Continue on the Sportsman Lake trail as it then drops down to the Gardner River. A crude but effective bridge gives access to the camp sites.

The following day it may be wise to leave the bulk of your gear hanging from the bear-proof pole before setting out. Head back up to take the trail up to Electric Peak. It is a good idea to get an early start as afternoon storms are common on the peak. It is also wise because there is little or no water available on the hike, so it's easier if the grunt work is done in the relative cool of the morning.

The trail roughly follows the ridge line, mainly in open sagebrush meadows with occasional dips into woodland, before steepening and leaving the lush woodland behind. As the ridge steepens, the trail follows fins of rock - if it gets too steep on the righthand side (east) try clambering over to the lefthand (west) side. Eventually, a short but impenetrable block of rock is reached not far below the summit. This needs to be turned on the left. You can either drop down slightly and cross the rock to gain a gully going up to the right, or more easily, drop down further to reach the same point without the exposure. Follow the gully back up to the ridge line and then carefully follow this to the top. There are numerous routes up from here, but all involve moving over very loose rock, so great care is needed, and watch that nothing is let loose on those below!

There is a summit register on the summit where you can leave your mark if you wish.

While on the descent, take care to remain on the trail as it is easy to miss the blazes. Don't forget to pick up your gear if you left it at the camp site.

Electric Peak.

The hike up Garnet Canyon. Bradley and Taggart Lakes in the background.

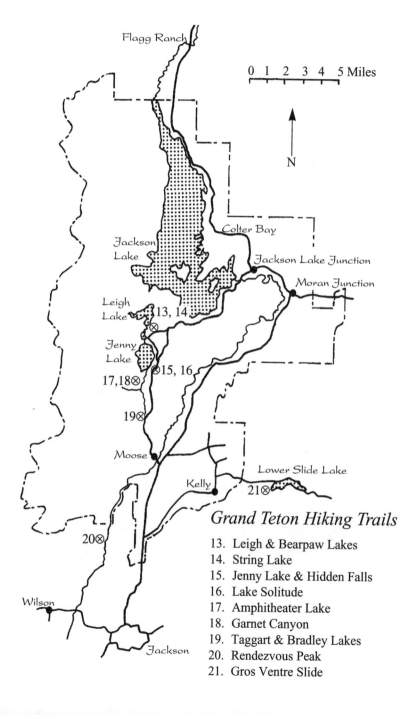

0 1 2 3 4 5 Miles

N

Flagg Ranch

Colter Bay

Jackson Lake

Jackson Lake Junction

Moran Junction

Leigh Lake   ⊗ 13, 14

Jenny Lake   ⊗ 15, 16

17, 18 ⊗

19 ⊗

Moose

Lower Slide Lake

Kelly   21 ⊗

20 ⊗

Wilson

Jackson

Grand Teton Hiking Trails

13. Leigh & Bearpaw Lakes
14. String Lake
15. Jenny Lake & Hidden Falls
16. Lake Solitude
17. Amphitheater Lake
18. Garnet Canyon
19. Taggart & Bradley Lakes
20. Rendezvous Peak
21. Gros Ventre Slide

13. Leigh Lake & Bearpaw Lake   `GT`

Distance: 6 miles	**Difficulty:** Easy
Time Required: 2hrs	**Terrain:** Good, level trail
Start elevation: 6,577ft	**Elevation gain:** 0ft
Best time of year: Summer and early Fall	

Unlike many of the lake trails in this section of the park, this trail can be remarkably quiet, although that is merely a relative term and it would be a rare occasion indeed to have the trail entirely to yourself. If you would like a quiet backcountry night in the Park, the sites around Bearpaw Lake are nice spots. Don't forget to book at the Ranger Station at Jenny Lake before setting out however.

The trails starts from the String Lake trailhead, which is located north of the Jenny Lake Lodge. Hike north following the edge of String Lake. This section of the trail is metalled and can be very busy. As usual, as you get further from the trailhead, the crowds thin out, and something of the flavor of this won-

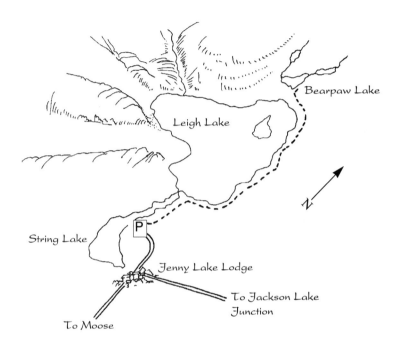

derful area becomes more evident. The trail stays mainly in the trees, but there are good views of the lakes and the mountains behind. When the lakes are still, particularly early in the morning, classic photographs can be taken of the reflection of the mountains on the lake surface.

As the trail follows the east rim of Leigh Lake, note the backcountry campsites and the precautions against bears looting the campers food. Bear proof poles and containers have been placed for this purpose.

At the north end of Leigh Lake the trail heads into a more open flat area to where the trail divides. The left fork leads up to Trapper Lake, the right to Bearpaw Lake. Go right and shortly after the lake is reached.

The return is back the way you came. To make the trail slightly longer, when you reach the north end of Leigh Lake, go right and follow the String Lake loop around the west side of that lake. At the south end of String Lake, go left (north) at the trail junction to bring you back to the parking area.

Opposite: Leigh Lake with Rockchuck Peak behind.

14. String Lake

`GT`

Distance: 3½ miles	**Difficulty:** Easy
Time Required: 1½hrs	**Terrain:** Well maintained trail
Start elevation: 6,877ft	**Elevation gain:** 240ft
Best time of year: Summer and early Fall	

The hike around String Lake is another popular trip which ranks highly for beauty, if not for solitude.

The trails starts from the String Lake Trailhead, which is located north of the Jenny Lake Lodge. Hike north following the edge of String Lake. The trail is initially metaled, and there are benches for the weary. At the north end of the lake the trail splits. The right fork continues on to Leigh Lake and then Bearpaw Lake. The left fork is the return route back along the west side of String Lake. Go left and cross the outlet of String Lake via a wooden footbridge to enter a wooded area. The trail then starts to ascend the hillside, gaining only about 240ft in the process. It then levels out and contours along above the lake.

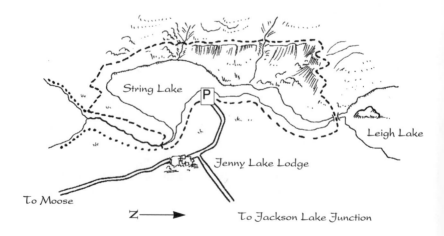

String Lake.

As you head south, the woodland thins out until you emerge in the open and a better view of the lake appears. A gentle descent leads back down to the level of the lake before the trail swings round to the east to join the trail that comes up from Jenny Lake. Take a left at the junction and head north back to the parking lot.

15. Jenny Lake & Hidden Falls

GT

Distance: 4½miles   **Difficulty:** Easy
Time Required: 2hrs   **Terrain:** Well maintained trail
Start elevation: 6,783ft   **Elevation gain:** 120ft
Best time of year: Summer and early Fall

The hike to Hidden Falls around the shore of Jenny Lake is one of the most attractive short hikes in the Park. However, it is highly popular and as a result can be unpleasantly busy during the summer. In addition, the erosion caused by the passing of so many feet is starting to seriously mar the beauty. Despite this, and in part due to the efforts of the Park Service, it is still worth doing, and is probably at its best during the Fall as the aspens hereabouts give a splash of color to the area.

Start from one of the parking lots on the shore of Jenny Lake, and find the trail heading to Hidden Falls. You will soon pass a jetty where a ferry can take you almost to the base of the Falls - if, of course, you were so inclined.

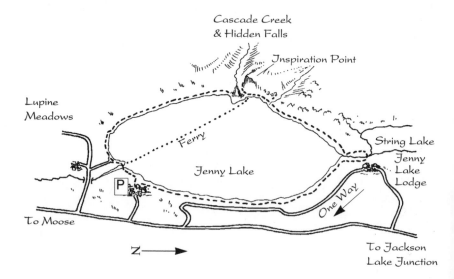

Jenny Lake.

Needless to say, you avoid the temptation and continue resolutely along the trail. The trail is basically flat, although rough in places. Once you reach the Falls, you can either turn around and come back, clamber up to Inspiration Point for more inspiration, or catch the ferry back across the lake.

16. Lake Solitude

`GT`

Distance: 15 miles

Time Required: Full day

Start elevation: 6,783ft

Best time of year: Summer

Difficulty: Moderate & strenuous

Terrain: Well maintained trail

Elevation gain: 2,267ft

Possibly THE classic hike in the Tetons, the trail to Lake Solitude is a long one, with ample reward at the end. During the height of summer, the trail can be busy, and some rather jokingly refer to the lake as 'Lake Multitude'. Try not to let that put you off, as it is still well worth doing. Note that the trail can be impassable due to snow into mid-summer. Check with the Park Rangers before setting out.

The trail starts from the Jenny Lake East Shore parking areas. The quickest approach is to take the ferry across Jenny Lake. There is a small charge for this. Alternatively, you can hike around the south side of the lake, this adds a further 1¼ miles. From the west shore boat dock, follow the well-marked, heavily travelled, trail up to Hidden Falls. Beyond this point the number of people drops

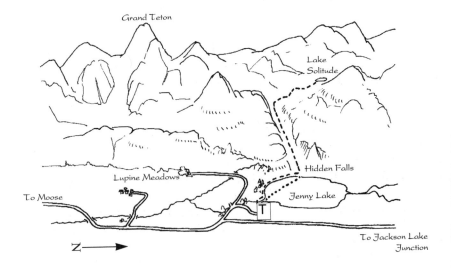

Hiking into Solitude Lake.

Photo: R. DuMais

dramatically. Climb steeply up the rocky trail to Inspiration Point, about a mile from the dock. Beyond here the trail climbs gradually as it follows the valley west on the right (north) side of the creek. After about another mile, you break out in to the open. The pond on the left was formed by an old landslide years ago.

The trail is now more open with good views of Teewinot and Mt. Owen on the south side of the valley. Roughly 2½ miles of easy walking bring you to a trail junction just the other side of a bridge over the North Fork of Cascade Creek. To the left, a trail goes up to Hurricane Pass. To the right, heading north is the trail on to Solitude Lake. Go right. A steady climb brings you out of the forest after about a mile in to a wide, open valley. In mid-summer, providing the snow has cleared, this area is covered by wild flowers. Continue on steadily for a further 1½ miles to reach Solitude Lake.

The return is the same way you came in. Note that the last ferry across Jenny Lake is at 6pm, so leave early if you intend to catch it!

17. Amphitheater Lake

GT

Distance: 10 miles	**Difficulty:** Moderate & strenuous
Time Required: Full day	**Terrain:** Well maintained, steep trail
Start elevation: 6,740ft	**Elevation gain:** 2,960ft
Best time of year: Mid to late Summer	

The trail up to Amphitheater Lake is a long, steep climb on a good trail to a great alpine location. Amongst its attractions are a profusion of wild flowers, and the possibility of seeing elk, deer, marmots and perhaps even black bears near the start of the trail. Early in the summer, snow can cover the trail for the final mile or so. There are also often steep snow slopes above the lake which should be avoided.

The trail starts from Lupine Meadows Trailhead, which lies just south of Jenny Lake, some 6 miles north of Moose on the Jenny Lake Road.

The trail starts from the south end of the parking area and heads on a level path through woodland. Height is gained gradually as the trail cuts through dense woodland, heading south.

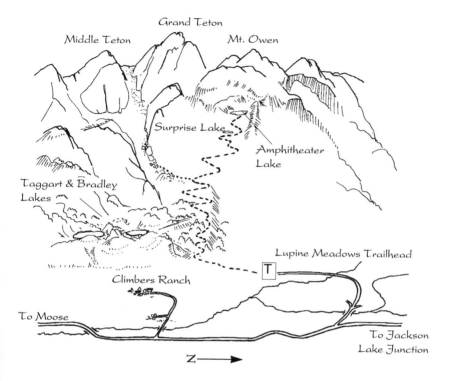

After about a mile the trail swings round to the west and climbs more steeply, with switchbacks, to a junction. This section is exposed to the sun, and is more pleasant if done early in the morning during the summer months. To the left is the trail to Garnet Canyon. Go right here to Amphitheater Lake.

The are many more switchbacks in the next 1½ miles as you ascend the steep, wooded hillside. Just before you reach Surprise Lake, the trail levels out. Circle round to the right of the lake, and carry on for a further ¼ mile, ascending gradually, to reach Amphitheater Lake. The lake is in a high, open cirque formed by glacial action and is surrounded by spectacular alpine scenery.

Return back the same way you came in.

Opposite: Amphitheater Lake.   Photo: R. DuMais

18. Garnet Canyon

`GT`

Distance: 10 miles   **Difficulty:** Moderate

Time Required: 5hrs   **Terrain:** Steep, well maintained trail

Start elevation: 6,740ft   **Elevation gain:** 1,300ft

Best time of year: Summer and early Fall

Garnet Canyon, traditionally the usual approach trail to the Lower Saddle, the start point for the most popular routes on the Grand Teton, is also a fine hiking trail deep into the Teton Range. One of the attractions of this trail is that it passes through dense forest, into open upland meadows notable for wild flowers, and on into mountainous terrain. It gets progressively steeper as it gets higher, and most parties would want to turn back before the Saddle is reached, if only as the final section is very steep, and can mean crossing steep snow fields early in the season.

Park at the Lupine Meadows trailhead, which lies just south of Jenny Lake, some 6 miles north of Moose on the Jenny Lake Road.

The trail starts from the south end of the parking area and heads on a level path through woodland. Height is gained gradually as the trail cuts through dense woodland, heading south. Black bears are not uncommon around here in the Fall as they feed on the berries in preparation for the winter.

After about a mile the trail swings round to the west and climbs more steeply, with switchbacks to a junction. To the right is the trail to Amphitheater Lake. Go left to Garnet Canyon. The open meadows hereabouts are a profusion of wild flowers during July and August. Due to their altitude, they flower later here than in the valley.

About a mile after the junction you arrive at the Boulder Field which lies within Garnet Canyon. The route through here is fairly complex, and some care must be exercised to avoid falls.

Finally The Meadows, a grassy alpine meadow area, is reached. This is a good place for lunch and then to turn around and head back down. Above here the trail is much steeper and less attractive.

Opposite: View up Garnet Canyon.

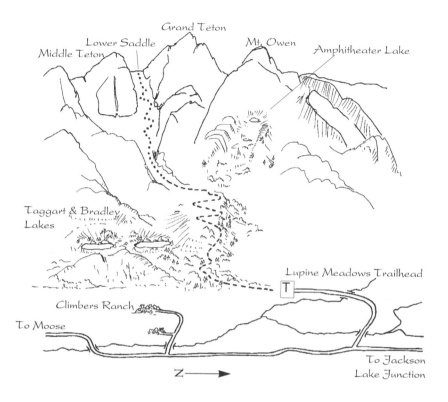

Middle Teton · Lower Saddle · Grand Teton · Mt. Owen · Amphitheater Lake · Taggart & Bradley Lakes · Lupine Meadows Trailhead · T · Climbers Ranch · To Moose · To Jackson Lake Junction · Z →

19. Taggart & Bradley Lakes

`GT`

Distance: 5 miles	**Difficulty:** Moderate
Time Required: 3 hours	**Terrain:** Good, well maintained trail
Start elevation: 6,653ft	**Elevation gain:** 467ft
Best time of year: Summer and Fall	

Taggart and Bradley Lakes, two lakes that were created by glacial movements, are popular hiking destinations, and for good reason.

Park at the Taggart Lake Trailhead 3 miles north of Moose on the Jenny
Lake Road. The trail heads across the flat open area from the trailhead towards
a low moraine bluff. Just before the edge of the higher ground, a trail is reached
that follows the line of hills. Take a right and head north. Initially the trail follows a level course past some cabins to a narrow ravine coming down the hillside to the west. Follow the ravine up on to the moraine bluffs. After about a
mile, a large boulder is reached where the trail divides. The left fork goes
directly to the shore of Taggart Lake while straight on takes you to Bradley

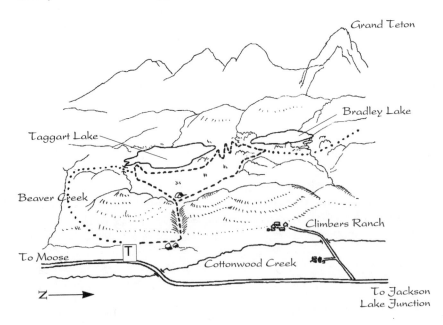

Porcupine. 3ft long, about 35lbs.
Lives on a diet of wood taken from directly under the bark of the
tree, as well as buds and twigs. Unique as the only quilled mammal.

Lake. Go straight and follow the trail as it gently climbs onto a ridge that separates these two lakes. Drop down the other side, and continue heading north towards Bradley Lake. Just before reaching the lake, a trail goes off to the left. This is your return route. For now, continue on to the lake shore and perhaps have lunch or a snack.

On the return, pick up the trail you past earlier, and take it to the right. (For a shorter return trip, ignore this junction and just retrace your steps). The trail climbs back up onto the ridge before dropping down via a zig-zag to follow a path close to the shore of Taggart Lake. Follow this south, until a bridge that crosses the lake outlet is reached.

From here you have two choices. The usual return is to take a trail that heads back east just prior to the bridge. This will return you to the large boulder met earlier, and back the way you came in. For a slightly longer trip, adding just under a mile, cross the bridge and take the Beaver Creek trail. It ascends the low ridge to the south of Taggart Lake before swinging round and down to the east to follow Beaver Creek to lower ground. After about a mile, it turns towards the north to return you to the trail junction just across from the trailhead.

20. Rendezvous Mountain

GT

Distance: 12½ miles
Time Required: Full day
Start elevation: 6,300ft
Best time of year: Summer

Difficulty: Hard
Terrain: Well maintained trail
Elevation gain: 4,150ft

Rendezvous Mountain is the peak on which some of the Jackson Hole Ski Resort lies. The Granite Canyon hike is long, mostly downhill on a good, well marked trail. Make sure you take water with you. The use of the tram to get up high makes this hike considerably easier. Note that because the top of the tram is 4,150ft above the valley floor, the weather up there can be very different.

Take the tram to the top. The tram operates all day at regular intervals. Tickets can be obtained at the clock tower in Teton Village.

From the top, go left (south-west) down a road along the ridgetop for a couple of hundred yards to a marked trail junction. Go right at the junction and

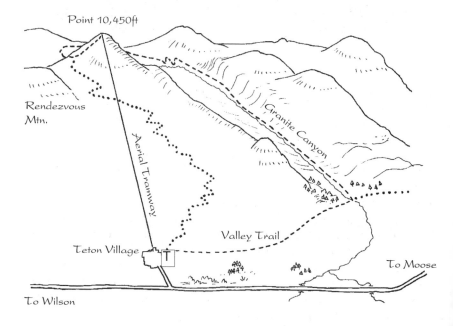

On the Rendezvous Peak Trail.

Photo: R. DuMais

descend across a small valley and up the other side, and over the ridge. Another trail junction is soon reached. Take the Granite Canyon trail which descends north for another 2 miles through open meadows into Granite Canyon.

Cross the bridge over a creek, past another trail junction and on to a National Park Patrol Cabin. Go right (east) and down into the Canyon. The trail follows the north side of the creek until it reaches a junction with the Valley Trail. Take a right, and follow the Valley Trail through woodland along the base of the mountains to reach Teton Village, in about another 2½ miles.

The alternative route back down uses the service road down the front of Rendezvous Mountain. This variation is about 7 miles in length and takes about 3 hours. From the first junction met on the ridge, go left (east) cutting back across an open bowl as the road descends steadily to the north, crossing the ski slopes on the east side of the mountain. Continue past the halfway house to almost the north edge of the ski area to where the road switches back to the south-east. Follow the road back into Teton Village.

21. Gros Ventre Slide

GT

> **Distance:** ½ mile
> **Time Required:** 1 hour
> **Start elevation:** 7,000ft
> **Best time of year:** Spring through Fall
>
> **Difficulty:** Easy
> **Terrain:** Maintained trail
> **Elevation loss:** 400ft

The Gros Ventre Slide is a piece of geological history that is unusual in that the main interest relates to an event that in geological terms happened minutes ago. The slide actually took place on June 23rd, 1925 and only lasted about 3 minutes. The debris pushed by the slide crossed the Gros Ventre River and formed a natural dam that led to the creation of the lake. The lake eventually burst through this dam on May 18th, 1927 and flooded the town of Kelly and immersed the town of Wilson (17 miles away) to a depth of 6 ft. Six people lost their lives in the flooding of Kelly. The dam was subsequently rebuilt, to form the existing Lower Slide Lake.

The area is of considerable interest, and this short hike, the Gros Ventre Geological Area Interpretive Trail, makes a fine outing.

To reach the slide, drive north from Jackson for 6 miles. Turn right (east) onto the Gros Ventre Road. A further 6 miles will bring you to Kelly. Follow the road as it turns and heads north for about a mile. Take the first right and drive for another mile to the Gros Ventre Geological Area Interpretive Trail parking area.

The huge scar on the southern slope of Sheep Mountain is the scoop left by the slide.

The hike takes you down to and loops around the rock debris that was once part of the slope. Here you will witness the remnants of one of the world's largest natural earth movements. It is a delightful excursion, full of interest with plenty of informative signs explaining the events and how they effected the local environment.

Opposite top: The huge scar left by the slide.
Opposite bottom: Some of the debris that was created by the slide.

22. Death Canyon

`GT`

Distance: 37 miles	**Difficulty:** Difficult and strenuous
Time Required: 2 - 3 days	**Terrain:** Steep, rocky trail
Start elevation: 7,000ft	**Elevation gain:** 3,800ft
Best time of year: Summer	

A magnificent backpacking round trip taking in the western and eastern slopes of the Tetons. Spectacular mountain scenery, great variety of flora and fauna and fascinating geological features make this hike a classic.

Note: A Permit is required for overnight trips in Grand Teton National Park. The easiest way to obtain this from the Idaho side is to visit the National Forest Office in Driggs to make the arrangements. They can contact the Park Service to arrange this for you.

From Driggs, Idaho, take the Grand Targhee Ski Resort road and then turn off at Teton Canyon for the National Forest Campground and parking area. follow the Alaska Basin Trail, gaining elevation gradually at first along the valley floor, then climbing more steeply into Alaska Basin. The Basin is a favorite backpackers campsite, although special care needs to be taken to protect this fragile environment. The Basin produces a profusion of alpine flowers in the Spring and early Summer as the snow thaws. This is a good place to camp if you wish to make this into a three day trip.

From the Basin Lakes the trail climbs more steeply to Bucks Mountain Divide (10,500ft), leaving the Jedediah Smith Wilderness Area and entering Grand Teton National Park at the Pass. It crosses talus fields then climbs using switchbacks to the Static Peak Divide at 10,888ft. From the Divide, follow the trail as it continues down the south spur of Static Peak and into pine forest, dropping 3,000ft, to reach a Patrol Cabin in Death Canyon.

There is a trail junction just past the Patrol Cabin. To the left, the trail continues down to Phelps Lake, and to the right is Death Canyon. Go right and follow the trail up the Canyon.

Find a suitable spot in the Canyon to camp the night.

The next day, continue on up the Canyon as it swings around to the southwest before climbing up to Death Canyon Shelf. Follow the obvious trail in a north-easterly direction for about 3 miles to reach the Mount Meek Pass

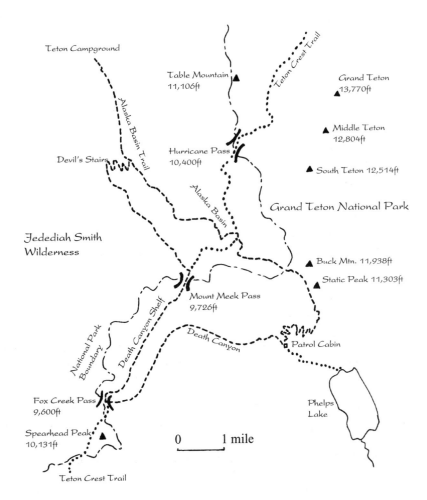

Note: Map for illustrative purposes only. Not intended for navigation.

(9,726ft). Along the way you'll find lots to keep your interest, precipitous cliffs to the west and east and for long stretches, near-perfect limestone paving.

Once over the Pass, swing off the Teton Crest Trail, heading north-west and losing height steadily towards the Devil's Stairs, which drop steeply into Teton Canyon. Once you have regained the Alaska Basin Trail, turn left (north) and follow it back to the campground from where you set out.

The impressive Death Canyon.

Photo: Trevor Twose

Hiking past Death Canyon Shelf.
Photo: Trevor Twose

Horseback riding in the Targhee National Forest.
Photo: Trevor Twose

HORSEBACK RIDING

The modern history of Wyoming is inextricably linked with horses. Even today, the horse plays an important role as a working animal on the farms and ranches throughout the region.

One of the original tourist attractions to the area, and in particular, the Jackson area, were the Dude Ranches which had their heyday at the beginning of the century. Some still operate, and offer a unique insight to the region.

The majority of visitors who get to ride horses in the area will go with an outfitter on a guided trip. These range from multi-day expeditions, which may be tailored for hunters or photographers for instance, through to shorter trips of perhaps a day or even less. The ultimate horseback riding trip in the area may be an overnight ride into the vast wilderness areas, with the outfitter arranging all the necessities of life. The outfitters can tailor your trip to your riding ability, with horses to suit pretty well any level. Certainly the first-timer may want to take a short trip to adjust to life in the saddle.

It is even possible to rent a horse for unguided riding in the region. This would entail riding from the rental location into the surrounding area, and you pay by the hour.

Both National Parks allow horse packing, and have regulations regarding this. As some trails may not be open to horseback riding, check with the Visitor Centers. The U.S. Forest Service produces a useful pamphlet called *Horse Sense* which covers horse packing in the backcountry. Contact one of their local offices for a copy.

The season for commercial horseback riding runs from May through September.

We have listed a few of the vast number of outfitters in the References at the back of the book.

A hunting day out in western Wyoming.
Photo: Lad Shunneson

H U N T I N G

Not surprisingly, the Greater Yellowstone Area offers some very fine hunting opportunities. Like almost all other national parks, Yellowstone does not allow any hunting. Grand Teton National Park, however, does, albeit very tightly controlled. This makes it quite unique in this respect, and of course, subject to some controversy.

The areas within this region where hunting is allowed offer an incredible array of opportunities for Wyoming's most popular trophy and big game species. The trophy game species, namely black bear and mountain lion can be legally hunted, and the big game species also available include moose, elk, bighorn sheep, deer and antelope. There are also the small game such as sage grouse, blue grouse, partridge, pheasant, wild turkey, cottontail rabbit and snowshoe hare just for starters.

The visitor to the region needs to be aware that hunting is strictly regulated in Wyoming, and licenses must be obtained before setting out. These are in great demand, and must be applied for well in advance. Compared to some other states, Wyoming Licenses are reasonably priced. For the novice, the regulations regarding hunting are complex and can be rather daunting. Contact the Wyoming Game and Fish Department for more information.

There are also outfitters in the region who will happily take you on a guided hunting trip. This may be the best way for a visitor to the region to get the most out of their trip, and enjoy the wilderness in the company of people who really know their stuff.

For help in choosing an outfitter, the Wyoming State Board of Outfitters and Professional Guides produces a free handbook that lists the licenced guides. It can be obtained from the Visitors Center in Jackson, or from the Board direct at: Wyoming State Board of Outfitters and Professional Guides, 1750 Westland Road, Cheyenne, Wyoming 82002.

How to Get The Most Out of Your Hunting Trip
by Lad Shunneson

Choosing A Guide

For a successful hunting trip, particularly in an area with which you are not familiar, the most important tip is to hire a guide. Don't just run through the Yellow Pages and pick out the first guide you come to. Instead, seek out recommendations from other hunters, or if that is not possible, contact different outfits and request several references from each. Some of the questions you might wish to ask the outfitters may include: Do they use horses? Are the guides knowledgeable about the locality in which you intend to hunt? What will your day be like? What kind of accommodation will be provided - is it a pup-tent, wall-tent or are there cabins? Is the cook good? What other amenities are available, if perhaps you are getting too sore to ride? Can you also fish? What is the outfits success rate? And ask to see any photographs they have of successful hunts.

The bottom line is to pay more and go with the best, rather than go on a cheap, badly run hunt.

Buying and preparing your gun

Buy a good gun and a good scope. Go to a good gun dealer, preferably one run by a hunter. Don't over-buy - too big a gun will produce a kick that will eventually make you flinch.

Well before you leave on your trip, get in as much gun practice as possible. Too many hunters go on hunting trips ill prepared, and consequently have a frustrating time. A hunting trip is not a good time to learn to use a new gun. If you are not prepared, then not only you will be disappointed, but also your guide. You will also have to return home in the knowledge that all your bragging before you went was in vain. Poor marksmanship also increases the chance that the game will be injured, rather than killed outright.

Choosing your game

Your choice of game may well influence your likely success rate. For instance, and providing you are with an experienced guide, you could expect a 100% success rate with antelope, deer may be 85%, and elk possibly 65%. Small game and game birds should not be overlooked as they can give very good sport, with a high likelihood of success.

Preparing for the trip

Make sure you pack plenty of suitable clothing for the trip. If you are heading into an area like Wyoming where the weather can be very poor, it is wise to pack plenty of warm clothing. A cold, wet, hunt without adequate clothing is a miserable hunt.

Finally

The most important part of a hunting trip should be the wilderness experience. The actual shooting is of secondary importance. If you go on the hunt with a view to enjoying the outdoors, in the presence of like-minded people, you are more likely to have a good time. In addition, if you have that attitude, you will be more relaxed and, consequently, likely to have a successful hunt.

Lad Shunneson, a professional guide and outfitter based in Boulder, Colorado, has provided successful outdoor adventures for sportsmen and sportswomen for more than 30 years.

Preparing to leave camp early in the morning.
Photo: Lad Shunneson

What a whopper!
Photo: Mark & Julie Springett

KIDS ACTIVITIES

There is so much to do in this region, it almost seems unnecessary to include a section on activities especially suitable for kids. There are however, a number of places that have something special to offer youngsters and they are collected here.

While many of the activities in this book can be done by children, it is a good idea if using an outfitter for something like rafting, to check to see if the intended trip is suitable for that age group.

The following places in particular welcome kids:

National Wildlife Art Museum, Jackson

The Art Museum has a 'hands-on' experience gallery called "Habitat For Young People". During the winter months, the sleigh rides into the Elk Refuge run from here and kids are welcome. Located just north of Jackson on the road to Grand Teton National Park. Tel: (307) 733-5771.

North Park, Jackson

Just north of the Visitor Center at the north end of town, a recently created park with a fishing pond especially for youngsters. Also known as Elk Pond. Visitors to the region must accompany their kids while they fish here.

Snow King Center Ice Rink, Jackson

An olympic-size indoor ice rink near the Snow King Ski Resort in town. Tel: (307) 733-5200.

Wilson Outdoor Ice Rink

Open to the public, lit in the evenings. Open during winter months only. Owen Bircher Park in the town of Wilson. Tel: (307) 733-5056.

Kids Club at Grand Targhee Winter and Summer Resort
Offers a variety of programs for infants through to 12 year olds. Tel: 1-800-TARGHEE.

Alpine Slide, Jackson
A 2,500ft long ride through the woods from Snow King Mountain. At the base of the Snow King Resort. Tel: (307) 733-7680.

Teton Valley Ranch Camp
Based in Kelly, just north of Jackson. Offers a week-long summer camp for kids, with a western theme. Tel: (307) 733-2958.

Alpine Golf
Also at Snow King Resort is a beautiful miniature golf course of 18 holes. Landscaped with waterfalls and ponds, a fun place to play and take in the spectacular views. Tel: (307) 733-7680.

Grizzly Discovery Center, West Yellowstone
A fascinating opportunity to observe grizzly bears and their young. Tel: (406) 646-7001.

Snake River Institute, Wilson
Hosts 'Snake River Summers', a series of activities for kids ages 6 through 15, during the months of June, July and August. Tel: (307) 733-2214.

Aerial Tram Rides
Running all year, the tram ride to the top of Rendezvous Mountain from Teton Village offers a birds eye view of Jackson Hole.

The ever-popular tepees at Dornan's in Moose

Opposite: Whoop Whoop!
Photo: Mark & Julie Springett

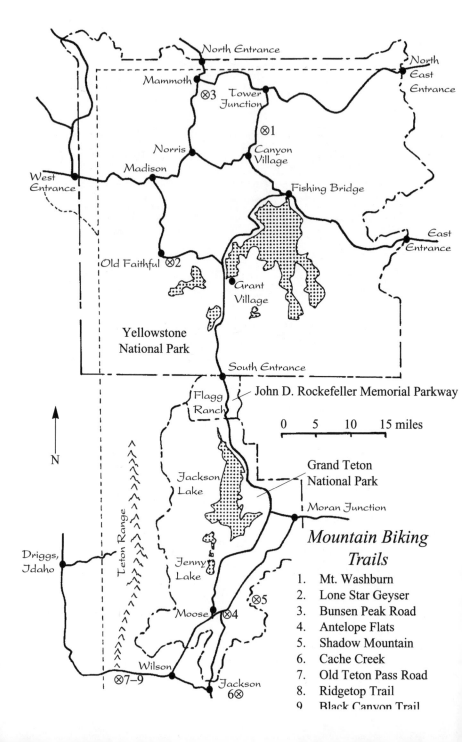

North Entrance

North East Entrance

Mammoth

⊗3

Tower Junction

⊗1

Norris

Canyon Village

Madison

West Entrance

Fishing Bridge

East Entrance

Old Faithful ⊗2

Grant Village

Yellowstone National Park

South Entrance

Flagg Ranch

John D. Rockefeller Memorial Parkway

0   5   10   15 miles

N

Jackson Lake

Grand Teton National Park

Moran Junction

Teton Range

Driggs, Idaho

Jenny Lake

Mountain Biking Trails

1. Mt. Washburn
2. Lone Star Geyser
3. Bunsen Peak Road
4. Antelope Flats
5. Shadow Mountain
6. Cache Creek
7. Old Teton Pass Road
8. Ridgetop Trail
9. Black Canyon Trail

Moose ⊗4

⊗5

Wilson

⊗7–9

Jackson

6⊗

MOUNTAIN BIKING

The mountain bike is possibly one of the finest machines ever invented for getting into the backcountry. There are, however, rules limiting its use in this region. They are for instance, banned from the backcountry in both National Parks, thereby severely limiting their usefulness here. Fortunately there are two rays of light. First, both Parks have opened up old roads to mountain bikes. These may not offer the mind-blowing technical difficulty that some may crave, but they do offer a surprising variety of trails. Secondly, the areas surrounding the Parks, in particular the National Forest areas around Jackson, do have much to offer the mountain biker - and some great technical rides to boot. The active mountain biking community in Jackson attests to the quality of biking in the area.

Throughout this area, whether in the Parks or not, you are asked to obey all signs, and stay on trails. Some of these trails will also be used by horseback riders. Always stop and let the horse and rider come past. In many ways, mountain biking in the whole of the West is on probation. It is up to the biking community as a whole to show that they are a responsible group of people. Irresponsible behavior will only lead to further restrictions on the sport, and that is in no ones interest.

We recommend all bikers carry a few essentials when out on these trails. These would includes: Water bottle - many of the trails are dry and dusty during the summer months, and drinking water hard or impossible to come by. Repair kit - containing patch kit for punctures, tire levers, pump and basic tool kit. Helmet - don't forget the bone dome, head injuries are so uncool. Food - perhaps an energy bar or two to munch on. Lightweight rain gear - storms in the afternoon are common and can come through very quickly.

Many of the trails are 6,000ft - 8,000ft above sea level and if you are not used to the altitude, take it gently on your first couple of rides.

1.   Mt. Washburn   YS

Distance: 6 miles	**Difficulty:** Easy but *very* strenuous
Time Required: 3 hrs	**Terrain:** Disused road
Start elevation: 8,840ft	**Elevation gain:** 1,400ft
Best time of year: Summer	

Mt. Washburn stands like a sentinel overlooking the Hayden Valley and offers two routes to the summit, of which only one, from the north, is open to bicycles. Following the old road to the summit, it is a challenge for even fit riders to get to the top without dismounting. This is more due to the effort required at this altitude, than to any technical difficulty.

The trail starts from the trailhead that is signed off the main highway as Mt. Washburn Chittenden Road. There is parking and restrooms here. Take the old road (now closed to vehicles) at the south side of the lot and begin the climb.

Once at the top you are rewarded with, if the weather co-operates of course, marvellous views all around. To the north you can see Electric Peak with its

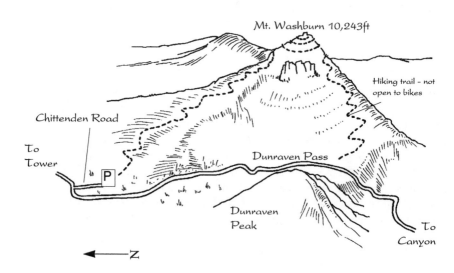

Matt on the summit of Mt. Washburn. Electric Peak in the background.

distinctive red cliffs, and to the south is Yellowstone Lake and the Hayden Valley. If you are lucky you will also see the resident herd of bighorn sheep that live on the rocky slopes of Mt. Washburn. The structure that sits on the summit is a fire lookout station (manned in the summer) as well as some communication equipment. There is also a room open to the public and restrooms.

The trip down is of course the main reason for the grunt up, and it is indeed a fun descent. Note that you must return the way you came up and stay on the old road. There are a few places on the road down where corners make visibility difficult, otherwise one can see well ahead to avoid other cyclists and hikers.

2.   Lone Star Geyser

YS

> **Distance:** 5 miles   **Difficulty:** Easy
> **Time Required:** 1hr   **Terrain:** Disused road
> **Start elevation:** 7,583ft **Elevation gain:** 55ft
> **Best time of year:** Summer and early Fall

Lone Star Geyser is perhaps one of the easiest backcountry geysers to get to. An old road leads from the Old Faithful to West Thumb road almost to the geyser itself. Following the Firehole River, it makes a fine family outing, or a gentle trip suitable for an after-dinner ride.

Park at the trailhead just south of the parking lot for Keppler Cascades on the Old Faithful to West Thumb road.

The trail follows the old road and route finding is never a problem. After crossing the river, it then follows it along a beautiful lush valley. It is quite possible to see bison and moose here. The road ends with a small open area, where bikes should be left, and then a very short walk brings you to the Lone Star

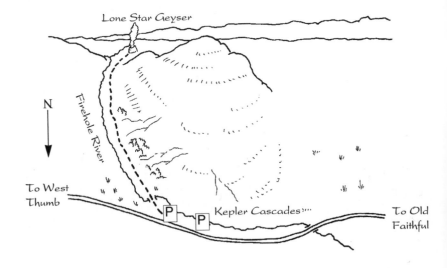

Lone Star Geyser.

Geyser. The Lone Star Geyser is notable for its 8ft high cone as well as its regularity (in 1994, it was erupting every 3 hours). It gives a fine display, best viewed from the road side of the open area. To help you calculate the time of the next eruption, there is a log book that is kept in a small wooden box on a stand near the geyser (the trick is to lift the lid of the box). If you witness the geyser erupt, note in the book what time it was so that people following will know how long they have to wait.

The river valley just beyond the geyser is often home to bison, and if you are passing the time waiting for the geyser, explore the area hereabouts, keeping in mind not to approach to close to the bison, and watch for small hot springs.

The return is back the way you came in.

3. Bunsen Peak Road & Osprey Falls YS

Distance: 9 miles   **Difficulty:** Moderate

Time Required: 3hrs   **Terrain:** Disused road & narrow trail

Start elevation: 7,400ft   **Elevation loss:** -800ft

Best time of year: Summer and Fall

The Bunsen Peak Road was until very recently open to vehicles, but is now closed and makes a pleasant ride through open woodland around the base of Bunsen Peak. In combination with a short hike to Osprey Falls, it makes a good outing. The cycling section of the trip is 6 miles total in length, the hiking section about 3 miles in total. It is possible to continue on the old road to descend down into Mammoth, but because the ride back up via the main road is not really suitable for bikes, we recommend this outing instead.

Park at the Bunsen Peak Trailhead just south of the Golden Gate Pass above Mammoth. The old road leads from the parking area following the edge of the higher ground, without really gaining any height. The road is still in fairly

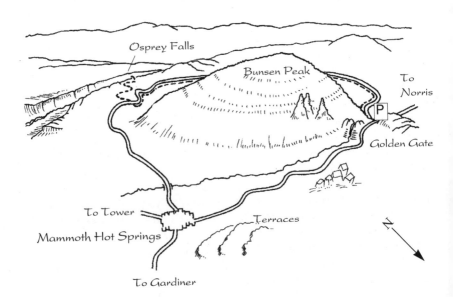

The old Bunsen Peak Road.

good condition, although it may be blocked in places by fallen snags, burnt in the 1988 fire.

Bunsen Peak towers over the road on the left. If you have the energy, the hike to the top is also worth doing. After almost 3 miles, a short steep descent leads to a small parking area on the right, with a metal bar for chaining bikes to. Lock your bike here (note that taking your bike to the Falls is prohibited). The trail follows the rim of the gorge, called the Sheepeater Gorge, in a southerly direction. The Gorge was named after a band of Shoshone Indians that once lived there. The river at the bottom is the Gardner, and is a fine fishing river which rises in the Gallatin Range, a remote mountainous section of the Park evident in the west from the parking area.

After a while, the trails starts to zig-zag down to the river. The trail is fairly narrow in places, but never too steep. As you descend down into the gorge, look across to the other side at the cliffs that have a well preserved basalt columnar structure. Similar rock structures can be seen elsewhere in the Park. A very short exposed section of the trail leads finally to the Falls. Not very remarkable, especially in a Park with so many waterfalls, they none the less make an attractive spot for lunch. Return the way you came in.

4.   Antelope Flats and Mormon Row   GT

Distance: 13 miles	**Difficulty:** Easy
Time Required: 2 hours	**Terrain:** Metaled & gravel roads
Start elevation: 6,660ft	**Elevation gain:** 0ft
Best time of year: Spring through Fall	

Antelope Flats is a easy ride on level terrain with historical interest, as well as fine photo opportunities of old farm buildings with mountain backdrops.

Park at the small trailhead one mile north of Moose junction on the main Jackson Hole Highway. There is a small crag here that is popular with local climbers. The Antelope Flats Road heads east away from the main highway here. Follow this through sagebrush with buck and pole fences. Views of rolling hills ahead, including Shadow Mountain, another good mountain biking destination.

After a 1½ miles, you pass the Mormon Road on your right hand side. Continue on to sad remnants of what were once the Pfeiffer Homestead build-

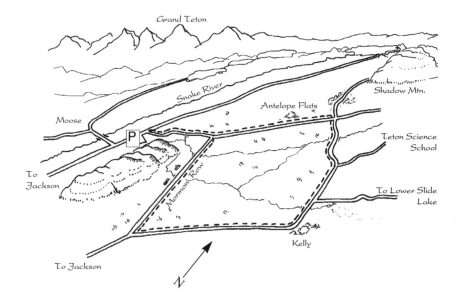

Picture perfect view of the Tetons from Mormon Row.

ings, circa 1910, destroyed in a fire in the summer of 1994. Soon after the Kelly road is reached. Turn right towards Kelly heading south. You will pass on the left a road going to the Teton Science School and another leading up to the Gros Ventre Slide. Finally Kelly is reached.

Leaving Kelly, you now head west. After two rather ordinary miles on metalled road, turn right (north) on Mormon Row. The road surface deteriorates to gravel for this section of the loop. Following a dead-straight path north, you pass the world-famous Moulton Barn which appears in many Grand Teton photographs and postcards. The Antelope Flats road is not much further on. Turn left to return to the parking area.

5.   Shadow Mountain Loop   `GT`

> **Distance:** 7 miles   **Difficulty:** Moderate
> **Time Required:** 3 hours   **Terrain:** Gravel road
> **Start elevation:** 7,020ft   **Elevation gain:** 1,370ft
> **Best time of year:** Spring through Fall

Shadow Mountain offers a panoramic view of the Bridger-Teton National Forest and is particularly picturesque during the Fall when the numerous Aspen trees cloaking the mountain start to turn.

From Jackson, head north on the main highway towards Moran Junction. Turn right onto Antelope Flats Road one mile north of the Moose Junction. Follow this for three miles to a four-way stop. Turn left, heading north towards Shadow Mountain. After about 1½ miles a wooded parking area is reached on the right.

To the right and just off the parking is a dirt gravel road signed 'Teton National Forest'. The trail begins here. Climb steeply through the aspens, glanc-

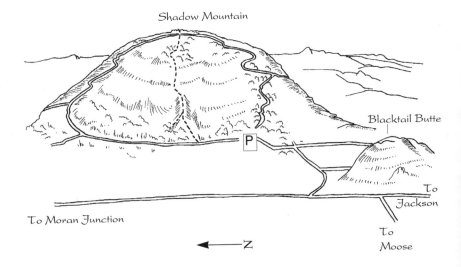

Ambling up Shadow Mountain.

ing back at least once to see a fine view of Mount Moran. The trail heads mainly east with several switchbacks and bends. It seems to take forever to reach the summit ridge. As you leave the woodland below, the Tetons appear on your left.

Head up the ridge going north for about a mile to the summit. Stop here for a well-earned drink and snack. To the east is the Bridger-Teton National Forest, where there is scope for further mountain bike exploration. Check at the bike shop in Moose for further information.

From the summit, the main loop continues north before taking a series of switchbacks down to the west to rejoin the Antelope Flats Road. Follow the road south back to the parking area.

Alternatively, there is a narrow single track trail heading due west from the summit that offers exciting technical riding. The trail takes a winding course on soft ground through woodland with a short steep uphill section appearing near the start. A junction in the trail is reached, take a left, and continue down. Watch out for several steep sandy sections with drop-offs. The valley bottom comes into view and soon after you rejoin the Antelope Flats Road. Note that this trail is open to horseback riders and care must be exercised during the descent.

Cruise for a mile heading south on the deeply rutted road back to the parking area.

6. Cache Creek / Game Creek Loop `GT`

> **Distance:** 18 miles   **Difficulty:** Difficult
> **Time Required:** 4hrs   **Terrain:** Mostly single track
> **Start elevation:** 6,344ft **Elevation gain:** 1,056ft
> **Best time of year:** Spring through Fall

An outstanding outing, one of Jackson's best. Starts and finishes in the town of Jackson, circumnavigating Snow King Mountain. A somewhat steep approach up to a col is followed by the reward of a lot of downhill riding with technical interest. A must for the aspirant hardman/woman!

Best done early or later in the day. Avoid the midday sun!

From the Hoback Sports store on Millward St. head south to Kelly Ave. and follow this to a deadstop sign. Turn right (south) on Redmond, then left on Cache Creek Drive. Head east on the multi-purpose road. There is a large trailhead parking area, with toilet facilities on the right.

From the trailhead, follow the road up Cache Creek (southeast). The road

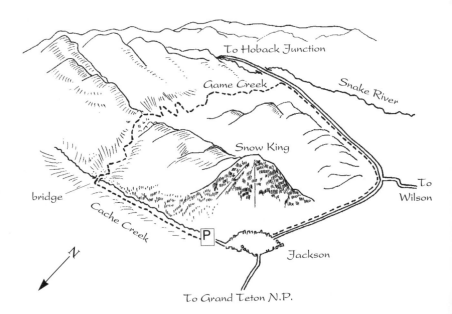

Crossing Cache Creek.

reduces down to single track after about 2 miles. A further 2 miles brings you to a bridge that crosses Cache Creek. Cross the creek and head steeply up what is now the Game Creek Trail to a col. There is a pleasant open meadow area here that makes a natural snack stop. The trail then continues through an area of windfall before opening out to reveal an easy, rock-less terrain, descent down into the Game Creek area. A fun 600ft descent on a narrow, sometimes twisting, dirt trail is the highlight of the trip. Definitely a hands-on-brakes experience for the faint of heart. Sadly it is over in a few short minutes.

Soon a fairly large lake appears on the right and provides a welcome scenic break. Dive through a small water splash and through a steel gate to reach another high meadow. Cruise through this, safe in the knowledge that the majority of the technical mountain biking is now over. The upper part of Game Creek Road is then reached. This is followed down to a junction with a metalled road. Turn right and follow it in a north-westerly direction to join the main Jackson highway.

Unfortunately the final section of this fine trail is a 50 minute jostle with the traffic north along this highway back into Jackson.

7.   Old Teton Pass Road   GT

Distance: 11 miles	**Difficulty:** Moderate
Time Required: 3 hours	**Terrain:** Metaled road
Start elevation: 6,635ft	**Elevation gain:** 1,916ft
Best time of year: Summer through Fall	

The Old Teton Pass Road is more than just a grunt up a hill. Offering a reasonable gradient, it is never too strenuous, and the rewards outweigh the effort required.

From Wilson follow the Teton Pass Road up towards the pass for 1 mile. Turn left at an obvious building called the Heidelberg onto a road signed to Trail Creek Ranch. Follow this for about a mile, past the ranch, to where the road is blocked. Park here.

Mount up and continue past the road block and on up the old road. It takes about 1½ to 2 hours to reach the pass. A small lake is passed on the right at about the halfway point. This is Crater Lake and is particularly picturesque dur-

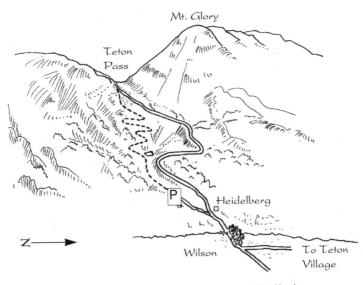

Cycling down the Old Teton Pass Road.

ing the summertime. The lake is a popular hiking destination and as a result, more foot traffic will be met on the lower section of the trail.

The road switchbacks six times for about three miles before the final section which parallels the Teton Pass Road above.

Once the Pass Road is reached, continue for a short distance on the main highway to reach the Pass. Find somewhere to sit and have a well-earned break.

The descent back to your car can be done quickly but to do it justice, take your time, watch for hikers and other trail users, and enjoy the scenery.

8.   Ridgetop Trail

`GT`

> **Distance:** 8 miles   **Difficulty:** Moderate
> **Time Required:** 2 hours   **Terrain:** Gravel road & dirt track
> **Start elevation:** 8,431ft   **Elevation gain:** 845ft
> **Best time of year:** Summer through Fall

A pleasant ride with technical sections that are never too difficult, making it suitable for families and beginners. Leads to a true summit offering excellent panoramic views. Note that this trail is at an elevation of over 9,000ft and is therefore not recommended if this is your first day at altitude.

Park at the parking area at the top of the Teton Pass. From the west end of the parking area, take the service road south. This takes you past a radio tower and on to the ridge.

The ridge trail is fairly smooth and only gently inclined. Follow it as it takes a path through several wooded and meadow areas and on up to a summit - named on maps as Point 9,279. The summit makes a nice place to picnic and

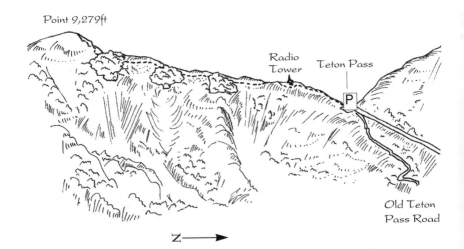

Looking back from the ridge to the Teton Pass Road.

take in the views.

From here, return the way you came in. Alternatively, the Black Canyon trail starts a short distance further on, and provides an exciting descent down to the bottom of the Pass. Note that it is a harder trail than this one however. See the next page.

9.   Black Canyon Trail   GT

Distance: 12 miles   **Difficulty:** Hard and strenuous
Time Required: Half day   **Terrain:** Road & rough dirt track
Start elevation: 6,635ft   **Elevation gain:** 2,615ft
Best time of year: Summer through Fall

A strenuous workout, the Black Canyon is a serious outing offering technical riding in a mountain environment.

From Wilson follow the Teton Pass Road up towards the pass for 1 mile. Turn left at an obvious building called the Heidelberg onto a road signed to Trail Creek Ranch. Follow this for about a mile, past the ranch, to where the road is blocked. Park here.

The first 5½ miles is a straightforward climb up to the Teton Pass. Once the Pass is reached, go to the west end of the parking lot and take the service road south. This allows you to gain the Ridgetop Trail which is followed on single track to Point 9,279. Just before the Point, bear right at a bench hewn from a

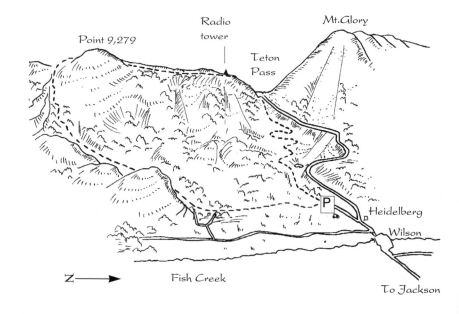

Descending into Black Canyon

windfallen tree.

Shortly after, a small sign nailed high on a tree indicates the start of the Black Canyon trail. The trail is obvious from here as it goes down to the left. The trail is rough and steep from here, with many rocks making the going difficult. The area around here is heavily wooded and the trail is fairly narrow so take care.

Swinging round to the east then north-east, the Black Canyon Creek is joined and followed for a couple of miles. It gradually levels out and becomes less heavily wooded before joining an old road. The road then heads north to join the Old Teton Pass Road which is then followed back down to the parking area.

Freddie tackles the 'V' on the Exum Ridge.

MOUNTAINEERING

In Wyoming, whenever mountaineering is mentioned, it inevitably means the Tetons. While Yellowstone has virtually no technical climbing, Grand Teton has been, for over half a century, this country's main center for the sport. Here you will find a wide variety of climbs of all types and grades, including many classics and routes steeped in tradition.

While all of the major peaks offer worthwhile climbs, the focal point for climbers has always been the Grand Teton, at 13,770ft, the highest mountain in the range. This is the most prominent and by far the most sought after Teton Peak.

In the history of American Mountaineering there have been few disputes as acrimonious and protracted as the argument as to who first climbed the Grand Teton. With the benefit of hindsight it is easy to put much of it into perspective, but at the time it received wide publicity. The first official ascent was made by N.P. Langford and James Stevenson, of the Hayden Survey, in 1872. They not only claimed to have reached the summit, via the Lower and Upper Saddles, but reported finding a small stone structure (the Enclosure) on the western sub-summit, the origins of which are also the subject of some conjecture.

On August 11, 1898 William Owen climbed the Grand with Franklin Spalding (who actually lead the entire climb), and two others, by what is now called the Owen-Spalding Route. Following this ascent Owen began a determined campaign to discredit the Langford ascent, as well as the one in 1893 lead by Captain Kieffer. The gist of his argument seemed to be that since he had not found any signs of these men, and that they had both described the Enclosure, therefore they must have merely reached that western spur. After several years Owen's deprecations were rewarded when he got the Wyoming legislature to recognize his expedition as the "official" first ascent, and to place a plaque on the summit honoring his effort.

Any climbing in Grand Teton National Park requires a permit and registration. Independent climbing is common place, but for those desiring instruction or climbing guides there are two sanctioned guide services. These are the only parties permitted to guide climbs in Grand Teton National Park and both offer a range of climbing opportunities, from basic instruction to difficult climbs and guided ascents of any of the routes and summits, including the Grand Teton. Their addresses can be found in the Reference Section at the back of the book.

Also, the American Alpine Club operates the Grand Teton Climbers Ranch, in Moose, from June to Sept. This facility provides a place to stay for climbers offering bunkhouses, showers, cooking area and so on, at very reasonable rates. It is a also a good place to meet other mountaineers. For more information contact: Grand Teton Climbers Ranch, Box 57, Moose, Wy. 83012. Phone: (307) 733-7271.

While many of the climbs can be managed in a day, it is not unusual for most parties doing the larger peaks to utilize a bivy or high camp. A permit is required for any overnight stay, and this can be obtained, as well as your climbing permit, at the Jenny Lake Ranger Station, which is also the best place to get up to date information on route conditions, weather reports and so on.

Climbing the Grand - A Primer

One can not over estimate the important position that the Grand Teton has held, and still maintains, in American mountaineering. Its appearance, history and numerous great routes all make it the most sought after technical peak in

Preparing to leave the Exum Guides hut on the Lower Saddle.

the country, perhaps only rivaled by Mt. Ranier in Washington state. This popularity remains high despite the fact that there is no non-technical route to its summit and that its ascent is a long and strenuous undertaking. And this popularity is applicable to experienced climbers and beginners alike.

A large percentage of the people who make it to the top are not experienced mountaineers, but "ordinary folk" who make the ascent with guides or experienced friends. But bear in mind that the Grand is no pushover. This is a serious alpine climb, with considerable dangers for the unwary or inexperienced. The summit is roughly 7,000ft above the valley floor and a base camp at the Lower Saddle is approximately 7 miles from the trailhead. Therefore, considerable effort is involved , and the weather can play a major role, with severe storms, involving rain, sleet, snow, lightning, high winds and cold temperatures at any time. But doing it is an ultimately rewarding experience, as any of those who have made its summit will attest.

Of the many, many climbs on the Grand, two are considered as the regular routes. These are the Owen-Spalding Route and the Exum Ridge. The Owen-Spalding was the original line, and is generally considered as the easier, in GOOD conditions, because the majority of the ascent is hiking and scrambling with only a short stretch above the Upper Saddle involving ropes and technical climbing. The Exum is usually considered a much finer climb, more aesthetically pleasing and enjoyable, with considerably more roped climbing.

Whichever way you go up there is really only one practical means of descent. This involves climbing down much of the upper part of the Owen-Spalding, and making a 100ft plus rappel, the lower part of which is free, and which does require two ropes. As is usual with an alpine climb, the descent is often the most hazardous time, as the climber is tired and more likely to make mistakes. While the Grand can be a fun, enjoyable experience, we once again want to stress the potential hazard involved in any such climb, as well as the importance of checking in and out with the Rangers.

Approach

While it is not unusual to climb the Grand in a day, most climbers will want to take two days to do the climb. The bivy sites at the Lower Saddle perhaps provide the best overnight spot for the popular routes to the top; although sites at the Moraine, or the Caves are often lest crowded, and more protected than the barren, windy Saddle.

The approach is via Garnet Canyon, and starts at the Lupine Meadows Trailhead. The trail (which is the same as for Amphitheater Lake for several miles) starts innocuously enough, but before long begins to climb steeply up a long series of switchbacks. After about 3 miles there is a junction, where the

trail to Amphitheater Lake goes to the right, and you should go left to Garnet Canyon, another mile further. At that point you scramble on through a short section of big boulders, where the trail may be difficult to follow.

Above that the route is obvious again, climbing steadily up the center of the canyon, to the Meadows at its upper end. Then the trail bears right, climbing steeply up zigzags to the Caves, situated at a fine viewpoint above Spalding Falls. Beyond this the route is all out in the open, continuing its long steep climb up the barren hillside before it levels a bit as it heads across the moraine. The trail climbing up to the right from this section goes to the Jackson Hole Mountain Guides camp which is high above, at the foot of Teepe's Glacier. Continue west up the moraine toward the Saddle, passing several bivy sites.

Just below the Saddle there is a tricky section, at a steep band or cliffs. At their right (north) end is a large fixed rope that makes it easier to scale this obstacle, and continue up the well-worn route to the Saddle proper. Here there are many crude bivy sites and tent cabins for the Exum Guides and rangers. There is a toilet on the west side, and a pipe for water on the east side, south of the path. Please use this just for drinking and do not clean utensils in that vicinity.

The Lower Saddle is also home to a veritable horde of thieving marmots, whose tenacity and bare-faced cheek is legendary. Most sites have a metal bar for hanging food from nearby boulders, and metal is about the only thing these opportunists won't chew up.

Whether from the Saddle, or a lower camp, most parties leave early for the climbs. As a point of reference, the guides are usually up and on their way before first light, and in general, the earlier you are up and off, the better.

The descriptions given here are for the Owen-Spalding, and Exum routes, the most popular and easiest lines up the Grand. But two things should be stressed. First, this a a general description of the lines, intended to give you a general reference to the routes. While for some this may suffice, others may want or need a more detailed or specific presentation. Anyone who has any qualms should consult one, or all of the technical climbing guidebooks listed in the back of this book. Secondly, the descriptions and grades given are for the climbs in GOOD CONDITIONS. The upper part of the Owen-Spalding Route faces west and north-west. Therefore it gets little sun, and during, and following bad weather it often ices up badly. This state can sometimes persist long after other sides of the mountain have cleared, so you should be prepared to encounter adverse conditions and adjust accordingly.

Matt on 'The Crawl' - a highlight of the Owen-Spalding Route.

The Owen-Spalding Route

From the Lower Saddle a crude trail heads up to the north, crossing a band of black rock (the 'Black Dyke') before entering a long gully on the left side of the prominent rock rib coming down from the Upper Saddle. A couple hundred feet up this gully is a prominent chimney gully on the right. Here the trail peters out and you have several options. Easy rocks on the right (south) of the chimney can be climbed to a ledge system that then leads back left to the top of the chimney. This route involves crawling through a short tunnel through some boulders - the Eye of the Needle, and an exposed step - the Belly Roll Almost.

Alternatively, or if the tunnel is blocked by snow, it is possible to continue up past the chimney, and then climb up and left across a slab to reach the ledges above the short chimney. This is exposed and some parties may want to rope up for it. Not far up the gully from the slab is a third alternative, a short, narrow chimney through a steep rock band. This is quite difficult, but often there are

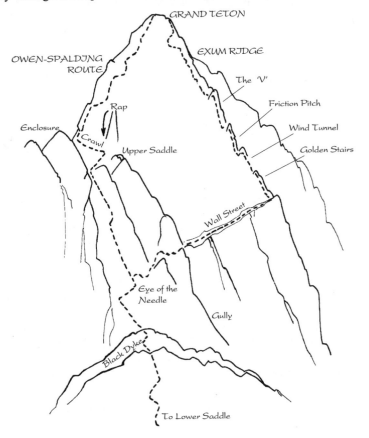

fixed slings that make this somewhat easier.

Whichever alternative you chose, beyond this the climbing is easier, and involves scrambling up along the rocks on the east (right) side of the gully. This can be exposed in places, but the higher you go, the easier it gets. Eventually you reach the Upper Saddle, a col between the broken rocks of the Enclosure to the west, and the steep cliffs of the Grand Teton to the east. The precipitous gully down to the north is the Black Ice Couloir, another popular route, so be careful not to knock rocks down into it.

From the Upper Saddle, after roping up, the climb goes north on ledges across the steep west face of the Grand Teton, and soon becomes VERY exposed as you traverse above the 2000ft drop to Valhalla Canyon. Pass a prominent chimney and a narrow spot (the Belly Roll) to the apparent end of the ledge. Continue on past another narrow spot (the Crawl) to a short, double chimney just beyond. This is the crux of the route. Climb the chimney, then follow the slabs and ledges that go up and right to the vicinity of the big rappel anchors. Then angle up and left up more ledges and short walls to the bottom of the 100' long Spalding Chimney, which is often full of ice. Climb up to the left of the chimney on steep rocks to its top. From there scramble a few hundred feet to the summit.

The Exum Ridge (Upper Section)

The classic route to the summit, the Exum Ridge is never too hard, but maintains technical interest most of the way, and with commanding views, it is never dull. It was first climbed by Glenn Exum (founder of the Exum Guides), and rivals the Owen-Spalding as the most popular line on the mountain.

From the Lower Saddle follow the Owen-Spalding until just above the Eye of the Needle. From there climb up to the right (east), to a notch on the crest of the ridge. Then traverse east, crossing the ridge and the wide gully beyond to the start of Wall Street, a huge ledge slanting up to the right toward the crest of the Exum Ridge. Reaching the ridge from the end of Wall Street requires roping up as it is very exposed, and is perhaps the crux of the route. Then go straight up a face called the Golden Stairs, to a step. Scramble along this and then up to the right, past a short steep, blocky section into the appropriately named Wind Tunnel.

Continue up the gulley above, mostly on its right edge, and up corners to the base of a steep slab. This is the Friction Pitch, one of the route's crux sections, and has little in the way of protection. Above that scramble up several hundred feet before crossing back to the left side of the ridge. Here you climb a big corner system (the V) for a lead to the ridge crest.

Scramble on up the ridge to a short wall and slanting chimney on the left

Matt leading the 'Friction Pitch' on the Exum Ridge.

side, which represents the last real difficulty. Beyond this a couple hundred feet of scrambling take you to a step where you can cross back to the right and go along snow to easy rocks on the right side of the ridge. These lead to the summit.

Descent from both Owen-Spalding & Exum Ridge

The only really practical descent is via a variation on the Owen-Spalding route utilizing a long rappel to the Upper Saddle. In bad conditions this route can be iced and messy. From the summit descend to the west and southwest to the top of the Spalding Chimney. Most parties rappel down this, from fixed sling anchors, as the rocks below are steep and usually icy. Continue down and to the left to an exposed viewpoint. The main rap anchors are just left of this.

A long rappel (100ft plus) that requires two ropes, takes you down to the Upper Saddle. From there slant down to the right (west) into a long gulley. Do not descend the gully to the left (east), which is closer to the Grand, and ends in cliffs below. The western gully and ridge goes down (trail in places) to the Eye of the Needle. This final short obstacle must be descended before a vague trail leads on down to the Lower Saddle.

Middle Teton - Southwest Couloir

After the Grand Teton, the Middle Teton, the third highest peak in the park, is perhaps the next most popular. The normal route up it is the Southwest Couloir. This is reasonable to do in a long day, but is easier from a camp at the Meadows in the upper end of Garnet Canyon. In early season (May/June), when there is considerable snow, it can be a straight-forward ascent on steep snow, using crampons and an ice ax. In late summer, when dry and free of snow, the couloir is a moderate rock scramble. In between, with sections of steep snow or ice, it makes a good introductory mixed alpine climb. In these conditions, crampons, an axe, a rope and a little rock gear may prove necessary. You should check with the Rangers when signing out to determine if these are needed.

From Lupine Meadows follow the trail to Garnet Canyon and up it to the Meadows, at its head. See the Grand Teton route description for particulars to this point. From the head of Garnet Canyon a faint trail leads up steeply into the South Fork, which is then ascended through boulder fields and across patches of snow or grass (depending on the time of year) to the saddle between Middle and South Tetons.

From there go north, up along the rocky ridge to the base of the prominent Southwest Couloir. This long gully system is then climbed all the way to its top. A short scramble brings you to the summit. The views of the south side of the Grand from this point are exceptional.

The descent is made by reversing the route. As stated above, in perfect conditions this is a straightforward ascent and descent, but in less than these the route can become considerably harder and more technical. As a general rule an ice axe and crampons should be taken if any snow is present, and a rope is advised as well if there is any question about conditions.

South Teton

The fifth highest mountain in the range, South Teton is also the easiest of the major peaks. Like any of them its ascent is a long and strenuous undertaking, and involves a huge elevation change. In good conditions an ascent of the South is never more than a moderate scramble, making it an attractive and reasonable goal for anyone in adequate condition. When a lot of snow is present the route does involve crossing steep, exposed slopes, and an ice ax and crampons are not only recommended, but at times may be essential for a safe climb. It is a good idea to check on conditions when registering, and heed the Rangers advice concerning conditions and gear.

The route is the same as the Southwest Couloir on Middle Teton as far as the saddle between Middle and South Tetons. See that description for information on how to reach this point.

From the saddle, hike up easy slopes to the south. These will be snow, or talus and tundra depending on the time of year. From the top of these slopes, near the ridge crest, go to the left (east) up along a steep rocky slope. In good conditions there will be a faint trail all of the way, but snow may obscure this and make the going tricky. This traverses above a steep ice or snow field, and reaches the base of a narrow gully. Go up this to its top and then continue up boulders and ledges on the south side of the peak to the summit.

The descent is straightforward, as you simply reverse the route up.

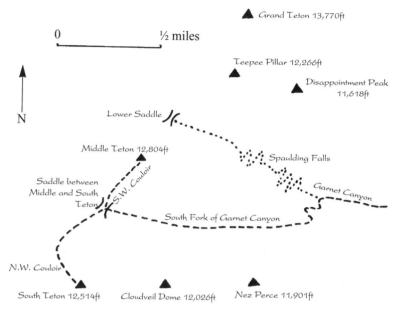

Above: Map showing routes to South & Middle Teton.

Above: Looking up the South Fork of Garnet Canyon towards Cloudveil Dome.

Opposite: Climbing the Southwest Couloir on Middle Teton.
Photo: R. DuMais

The start of a perfect flight.

PARAGLIDING

Imagine hiking up a hillside or mountainside then unfolding your paraglider (simply a high-tech parachute weighing about 15lb) on the ground. A quick tug on the control lines and almost instantaneously you have a flying machine literally at your finger tips. An upward glance at the paraglider to ensure all is well, and away you go. Relax back into your seat harness and enjoy the thrill. Initially your flights may be modest, just down to the foot of the hill, but with practice and experience, you can fly further and for longer.

A common misconception is that the pilot JUMPS off the mountain. WRONG! Rather, the canopy is inflated into the wind by running down an incline. This is why the foothills are used. The speed of your run, combined with the head-on wind give the paraglider the airspeed it needs to lift the pilot up. In lighter winds, the pilot will need to run faster, in stronger winds, the run may be only a couple of steps. Once in the air, the sensation tends to be one of tranquility.

The best and safest introduction to the sport is through a recognized school. Most schools will take you for just a one day introduction course. Some schools offer tandem instruction, that is, where you fly with the instructor under the same canopy. Tandem flying is a great introduction to the sport and allows you to get airborne much quicker. Also, because the pilot is very experienced, you will probably get a longer flight than would be normal on your first day of training.

While a full Certification Training Course (Class One) is a multi-day learning experience, the average student should be flying short distances during his or her first day of paragliding. Class One Certification is the minimum requirement for flying at most registered sites across the country.

The sport of paragliding is administered by the US Hang Gliding Association (USHGA) based in Colorado Springs, which registers pilots and sets out policy for training and qualifications. Also, as the sport is recognized as aviation, it comes under Federal Aviation Authority (FAA) regulations and Rules of the Air.

Generally the sport is very safe, although as it is a form of aviation, it is important to take it seriously. We recommend that beginners approach an established school for flying instruction.

To our knowledge, paragliding seems to be a significant activity only within the Jackson area. There are several good sites, with a small but active group of local pilots. During the summer months there is a period when early evening "magic air" provides very smooth yet buoyant flying with great possibilities for height gain and cross-country.

We have not listed flying sites here because we feel it is important for visiting pilots to get in touch with local pilots. This is the best way to get up-to-date information regarding the sites, access to them, and weather conditions. As is the case with flying elsewhere in the USA, arming yourself with local knowledge is the best way to avoid conflicts with landowners and local residents.

Currently, paragliding, like hang gliding, is banned in the National Parks. Flights have been made from the summit of Grand Teton, but this is not only illegal, it is an extremely serious proposition as well.

There is a school operating in Jackson that offers courses, from one day 'tasters' through to certification courses. The school is also a good point of contact for visiting pilots. See the reference section for more information.

Opposite: Idyllic paragliding days in the Jackson area.

Floating the Snake River.
Photo: Barker/Ewing River Trips

R A F T I N G

If someone offered you a chance to view some of the world's most impressive mountains, see wildlife such as elk and moose in their natural settings then throw in a sumptuous meal of steak or trout with fresh salad, watermelon etc, you'd think they are talking of an exclusive holiday in an exotic country miles away. In fact they are probably talking about rafting the Snake River!

The Snake is the most popular floating river in the area, although there are other, equally fine rivers within a short drive. The Snake has a diverse range of water trips, including mellow float trips, whitewater rafting and fishing trips. There are a vast number of companies operating in the Jackson Hole area who can offer pretty much any type of river trip you could ask for. Typically, the shortest trip will last about 2 hours including travel to and from the river. Longer trips are also offered, some even overnight. Perhaps the most interesting day trips are those that start early in the morning as this is a good time to see wildlife along the river banks. Alternatively, a late afternoon trip followed by a steak dinner is a also fun.

For the more independent spirits, it is possible to rent river craft. Available are a wide range of boats, from simple one-man kayak-type through to large rubber rafts that will need you to supply a team of people. If you are such a type, bear in mind that sections of the Snake River are not suitable for novices. Check the Water Sports section in this book for more information and regulations that need to be observed.

While it seems fun to take a camera along, bear in mind that some trips will carry you through wild water, where you will probably get wet. Unless you have a waterproof camera, or camera bag, you might want to leave it behind. For those 'once in a lifetime' shots, you could always arrange for a staff photographer to take photos of you from the shore. Check to see if this service is available when booking.

Commercial river rafting does not take place in Yellowstone National Park.

Hitting the highway in Wyoming.
Photo: Chuck Anderson

ROAD CYCLING

While this area has so much to offer visitors, it cannot be said to be prime road-cycling country. This is because the highways tend to be narrow and very congested, making it less than optimal for touring. That is not to say that it is impossible, (see Chuck's account below) it is just not for the faint of heart, and cannot be recommended for families. There are quieter roads, but they are a rarity. The Mountain Biking Section does include disused highways that could be ridden on a road bike, although they tend to be short in nature.

The best time to ride in the area would either be before Memorial Day, weather permitting, and after Labor Day. This would ensure that the roads were relatively quiet. Some campgrounds do have sites specifically reserved for hikers and bikers without vehicles. You are very unlikely to get turned away, even when the campground is very busy, if you arrive under your own steam.

Because of the distances involved, you should always carry some basic tools and spare bicycle parts, and as with any activity, take plenty of water. A helmet should be standard equipment, and watch out for those extended side-view mirrors on RV's and campers.

Cycling through Yellowstone and the Tetons
An Account by Chuck Anderson

One of the best ways to see this area is from a bicycle. The silence, solitude, and awareness can not be had from a motorized vehicle. On a recent cycling tour (1994) I entered the park from West Yellowstone, in Montana, and camped two nights in Yellowstone at Madison Junction and Grant Village. The third night I spent in a lofty, secluded, campsite east of the Teton range.

Yellowstone is known to cross-country cyclists for it's narrow, decaying, busy roads. Yes, the road is in deplorable shape, and the traffic is heavy, with many large campers driven by novice drivers. Yet I, did not feel threatened on my ride through the park. In fact, I consider it to be one of the most beautiful, and by far the most interesting stretches of road I encountered on my journey from Seattle to Boulder. Cycling in Yellowstone can be very pleasant with a little care and planning.

The road from West Yellowstone to the Madison Junction campground is new and has smooth, wide (safe) shoulders. Almost all of the trees along this route were denuded by the fires of 1988. As the ranger at the entrance gate had told me, I found Riverside Dr. four miles inside the park. It is a short, but blissful alternate to the main road. It adds no extra mileage and it would be a shame to miss it.

One very nice thing about Yellowstone National Park are the guaranteed campsites for hikers and cyclists. At Madison Junction, there is a hiker/biker area near the ranger's cabin where cyclists and hikers can set up camp. There are benches and firepits to share and always enough room for one more. The ranger at Madison Junction even let me chill down a few beers in his fridge. There are restrooms, but no showers at Madison Junction. However, the Madison river, formed by the junction of the Firehole River and the Gibbon River, runs by the camp. It has a swift, but manageable current and streams of warm water swirling through it that are heated by Yellowstone's famous geothermal energy. You can't use soap, but some time spent in the river will leave you pleasantly refreshed. And you'll get to meet some of your fellow campers.

On the Firehole Canyon Loop in Yellowstone.
Photo: Chuck Anderson

The road from Madison Junction to Old Faithful is old and broken up in some places. There is virtually no shoulder. Remember to take the Firehole Canyon loop, as it is another pleasant alternate to the main road. Although the road is in such bad shape, I never felt too threatened. Nearly every driver was courteous and patient, slowing behind me until it was safe to pass. Recommendation: leave Madison Junction campground very early (by 7 or 8 AM) to avoid most of the traffic and sightseers at the Lower and Middle Geyser Basins. The scenery along this road is almost surreal.

A stop at Old Faithful is worthwhile. Wading through the tourists, you can find a decent lunch and stay long enough to see the Old Faithful geyser send it's hot, steamy spray surging hundreds of feet into the air.

The road from Old Faithful to Grant Village is much like the morning's route, but not as decrepit, and, again, the motorists were, for the most part, patient and courteous. Before descending towards beautiful, blue Lake Yellowstone you cross the continental divide three times. The highest point reached is actually on a hill between these two crossings.

Grant Village is much like Madison Junction. There are several campsites set aside for and to be shared by cyclists and hikers. There are no showers in the campground, but just a stones throw from the entrance is a convenient commercially run laundry and shower facility. After washing clothes and showering (ahhhh) my assigned camp partner and I rode into the village and had a steak dinner in a cafeteria by the lakeside. It was a little too expensive, but much easier than cooking at camp, and a delicious, well deserved luxury.

The next day I left Yellowstone, heading south towards Grand Teton National Park on the John Rockefeller, Jr. Memorial Parkway. The road was the same - narrow and busy. I've learned to ride these roads assuredly by being courteous and allowing traffic plenty of room to pass. For much of the ride, though, there was no traffic, and the scenery along the Lewis River is beautiful with dramatic canyon overlooks. Looming ahead are the Tetons.

I entered Colter Bay, where I was thinking of camping that night, and found it to be much like Grant Village, with shops and a large RV campground. The hiker/biker sites at Colter Bay are secluded and removed from the rest of the campsites. But, straddling my bike, waiting in a line of RV's to register for a campsite, I realized that I'd had enough of the comfort, noise, and crowds of a large campground and decided to head for a hiker/biker only campsite, just past Moran Junction - east of the Tetons and Jackson.

The first night I spent alone in bear country, three nights earlier, was in the Beaver Creek campground near Earthquake Lake and Hebgen Dam, in Montana, west of Yellowstone. There were no bear boxes, just bear-proof trash cans, and I was alone in a dark and secluded site. There was no one else within a hundred yards of me and, in the darkness of a new moon, I got jumpy. I called it a night early and cowered under my sleeping bag in my tent.

Spending the next night at Madison Junction, with lots of company, was a welcome relief. There were bear boxes and a virtual city of campers parked nearby - somewhat noisy, but reassuring. At Grant Village there was much of the same. Plenty of company and bear boxes, so that all food and odorous items could be kept locked away from where I was sleeping in my nylon tent. On this last night, I would be alone again and in a very secluded spot.

Leaving Colter Bay I rode to the junction with Highway 287 and headed east towards Moran Junction and Togwotee Pass. Four or five miles into the climb, just past the 12 mile marker, 13 miles east of Moran Junction, was the entrance to Blackrock Bike campground. Blackrock was set up by the Adventure Cycling Association and the National Forest Service. It is a cyclist-only campground overlooking the Teton range. There are benches, firepits, and bear boxes. Firewood is abundant and lying dead on the ground. There's even a two-seater outhouse. There is no water available at the site, but I stopped at a motel about 5 miles before the campground for food, water, and ice. There's also a KOA campground further back toward Moran Junction.

This is the finest campsite a cyclist could wish for. Seclusion and a view. The campsite is on the side of a hill facing east. Five hundred feet below is the valley floor and twenty miles west is the entire Teton range, in full view. After judiciously keeping a clean campsite and locking away all food and toiletries in a bear box I had the most pleasant, worry-free camping experience of my entire trip.

When some rangers came in the morning to empty the trash they said that the site may get moved back down the hill adjacent to a drive-in campground due to lack of use. What an abhorrent thought. You should check ahead of time. Call Adventure Cycling in Missoula Montana (406-721-1776) for the latest information. From this campsite, I saluted the beautiful Teton mountains and headed east over Togwotee Pass and into dry, desolate, windy, central Wyoming. But that's another story.

Cycling the Jenny Lake road in early Spring.

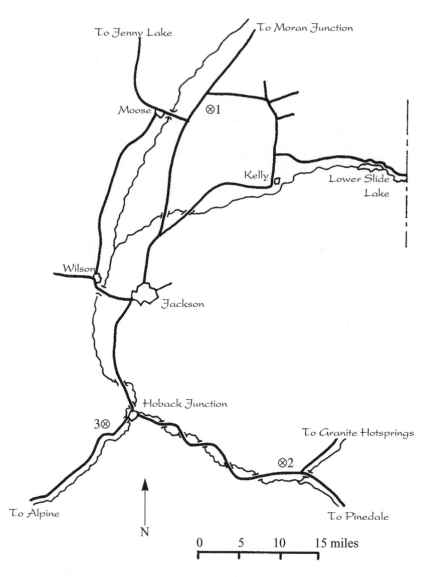

Sport Climbing Crags in the Jackson Region
1. Blacktail Butte
2. Hoback Shield
3. Rodeo Wall

R O C K   C L I M B I N G

The importance of mountaineering in the Tetons tends to overshadow the rock climbing possibilities in the area. Yellowstone does not present anything of real interest to the climber, as the outcrops there are small, often remote, and the volcanic rock is of poor quality. For this reason, climbing is discouraged in Yellowstone by the Park Service. In Grand Teton National Park however, there is a lot of rock, but again, much of it is remote and involves long approaches. Registration is required for any climbing in the National Park.

However, that does not mean that Jackson Hole is devoid of interest to the rock climber. In Grand Teton National Park there are many good rock climbs. Some of the classic climbs are: Guide's Wall, The Snaz, Irene's Arete and the South Buttress Direct and the South Buttress Right on Mt. Moran. These all have fairly long approaches and are in an alpine setting. One of the closest traditional rock climbs is Baxter's Pinnacle which we have described overleaf.

The region also boasts three fine sport climbing style crags which are gaining in popularity. All of the climbs are steep and strenuous, very much in the modern idiom. Topos and information about these are given in this chapter.

Good, but limited, bouldering can be found on the east side of Jenny Lake, just west of the campground and at Bouldertown, off the road to String Lake. There is also good rock climbing on the west side of the range too, just above the Teton Canyon trailhead. For more information on these climbs, and the climbing or bouldering areas, consult one of the guidebooks listed in the back of this book.

In the town of Jackson, one finds the Teton Rock Gym, an indoor climbing facility, at 1116 Maple Way. Phone (307) 733-0707. This is open daily and offers lessons and rentals.

Rock climbing is one of those activities in which it is ridiculously easy to get into difficulties. We strongly urge beginners to learn the basics of the sport through an indoor climbing gym or one of the local climbing schools.

On Baxter's Pinnacle.

Photo: R. DuMais

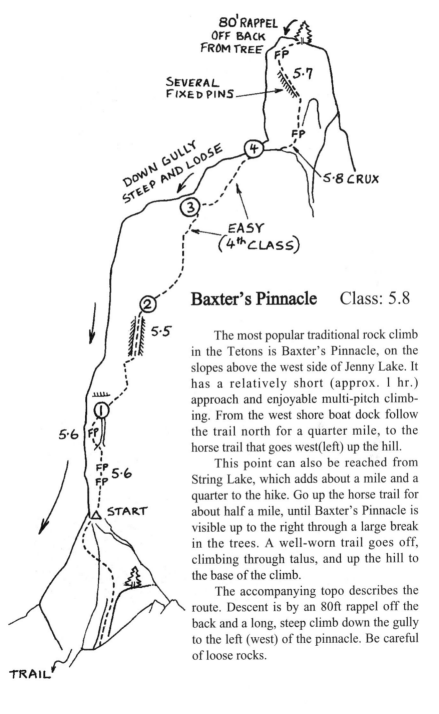

80' RAPPEL OFF BACK FROM TREE

FP

5.7

SEVERAL FIXED PINS

FP

DOWN GULLY STEEP AND LOOSE

④

③

5.8 CRUX

EASY (4th CLASS)

②

5.5

① FP

5.6 FP

FP 5.6

△ START

TRAIL

Baxter's Pinnacle   Class: 5.8

The most popular traditional rock climb in the Tetons is Baxter's Pinnacle, on the slopes above the west side of Jenny Lake. It has a relatively short (approx. 1 hr.) approach and enjoyable multi-pitch climbing. From the west shore boat dock follow the trail north for a quarter mile, to the horse trail that goes west(left) up the hill.

This point can also be reached from String Lake, which adds about a mile and a quarter to the hike. Go up the horse trail for about half a mile, until Baxter's Pinnacle is visible up to the right through a large break in the trees. A well-worn trail goes off, climbing through talus, and up the hill to the base of the climb.

The accompanying topo describes the route. Descent is by an 80ft rappel off the back and a long, steep climb down the gully to the left (west) of the pinnacle. Be careful of loose rocks.

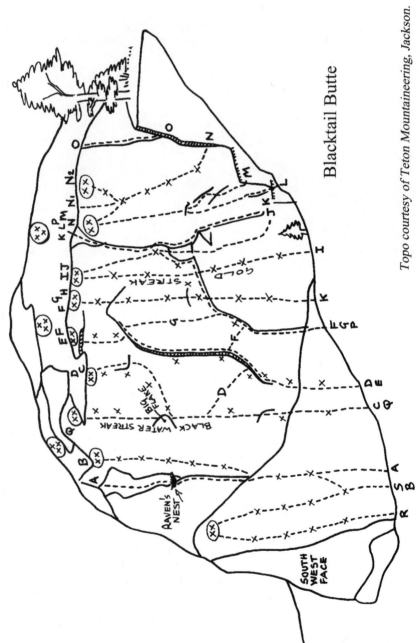

Blacktail Butte

Topo courtesy of Teton Mountaineering, Jackson.

A. Raven Crack 5.9
B. Do The Right Thing 5.11c
C. Waterstreak 5.12a
D. Connect 5.12a
E. Arch Direct 5.12b
F. Regular Arch 5.12a
G. The Squeeze 5.12c
H. Kehoe Kling 5.12b
I. Jingus Road 5.12a
J. Your Route 5.12b
K. Breashears Route 5.12b

L. Monster Route 5.13a
M. Diagonal Crack 5.11a
N. Step Out 5.9
N_1. variation 5.10b
N_2. variation 5.10c
O. Right Crack 5.9
P. Bolt Route 5.11a
Q. Waterstreak Direct 5.12c/d
R. As You Wish 5.11b
S. Inconceivable 5.10d

Blacktail Butte

Ten miles north of Jackson, on the east side of Highway 89, is Blacktail Butte. From the parking area just north of the Moose Junction, a trail leads easily to the base of the main cliff, which is about 50ft high.

Once a top-rope area, most of the lines have been retrobolted so they can also be led.

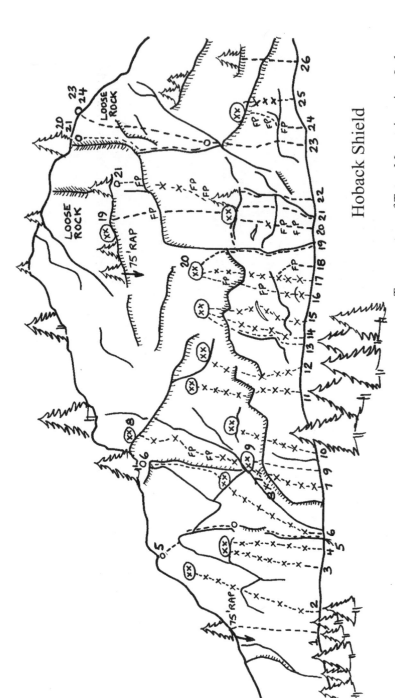

Hoback Shield

Topo courtesy of Teton Mountaineering, Jackson.

1. Toprope 5.8
2. Petzl Logic 5.10
3. A Thousand Cranes 5.9
4. The Joker 5.10
5. Malvado Edge 5.8 (1st), 5.9 (2nd)
6. Muff Buster 5.10c (1st), 5.9 (2nd)
7. Electric Shower 5.11c (1st), 5.10d (2nd)
8. Electric Shower Variation 5.11a
9. Toprope 5.12b
10. She's Gotta Have It 5.10c
11. Dengue Fever 5.10d
12. Fandango 5.10c
13. The Hunter 5.9

14. Naughty Guides 5.10a
15. La Bamba 5.10a
16. McFlatus Roof 5.10c
17. Nherrvus Sheep Direct 5.11b
18. Nherrvus Sheep 5.11a
19. The Bulge 5.8
20. Deception 5.10c (1st), 5.8 (2nd)
21. Patty's Butt 5.9
22. First Lead 5.8
23. Hookit 5.9
24. Jam Or Slam 5.9
25. Bolt Face 5.9
26. Toprope 5.5

Hoback Shield

The major sport climbing crag is the Hoback Shield, which has the largest number of routes, most of which are bolt protected and about 70ft-90ft long. This is 24 miles south of Jackson on Highway 189, just before the Granite Creek turnoff. A well-worn trail leads several hundred yards up the hillside to the cliff.

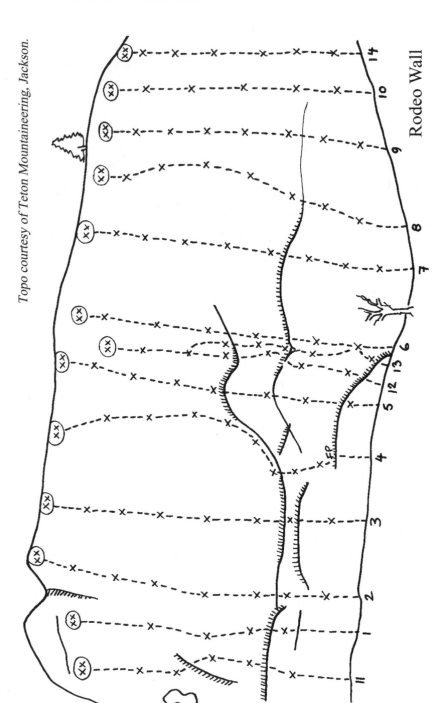

Topo courtesy of Teton Mountaineering, Jackson.

Rodeo Wall

1. Quickdraw McGraw 5.10a
2. Bulldog 5.11b
3. Ten Second Ride 5.10c
4. Cowgirls Wear Chaps Only 5.11a
5. Buck Dancer 5.10c
6. Copenhagen 5.10a
7. I Against I 5.10a

8. Betty Tendon Blaster 5.9
9. Thelma 5.9
10. Louise 5.10a
11. Alive In Wyomin 5.10a
12. Wanna Be A Cowboy 5.10c/d
13. Redman 5.10
14. Rodeo Queen 5.8

Rodeo Wall

The Rodeo Wall is 2 miles south of Hoback Junction, on Highway 89 to Alpine. Located on the west side of the highway. A good trail leads to the crag which is only a few minutes from the road. There are quite a few steep, bolted face climbs, 60ft-90ft long.

The Lame Duck Limp. Steve Thomas leading,
and eventually winning!
Photo: Jackson Hole Guide

R U N N I N G

This region has some of the finest running trails to be found anywhere in the US. The dramatic scenery and wildlife add a touch of uniqueness not found anywhere else. There are trails for just about all levels, from disused highways, through to meadows and on up to high mountain trails.

The Jackson Hole area sports a number of competitions, again for all levels, and these are organized by the local running club that is based in Jackson. This small, but energetic club, called the Jackson Hole Road Runners Club, welcomes visitors and newcomers. The races range from a 5km run/walk right through to the Moose Chase Marathon. For the marathon, all runners who have trained at high altitude, and can reasonably expect to finish within 6 hours are eligible for entry. The races are run from May through to September. A schedule can be obtained from the Jackson Visitor Center or direct from the Club. The Club can be contacted at (307) 733-2720.

Popular trails in the region include in Yellowstone, the disused highways that go into Lone Star Geyser and the Fountain Flats Drive, as well as the hill climb up Mt. Washburn. Running around the geyser basins cannot be recommended due to the danger of slipping and falling into the hot springs.

In the Jackson Hole area, trails such as the Valley Trail that goes from Teton Village up to Jenny Lake, and the Cache Creek Trail are popular. There are also, for the experienced runner, great mountain runs. The run up Snow King Mountain just outside of Jackson is popular with locals for an early evening run.

You are warned however, particularly when running through woodland, to beware of frightening wildlife. Bears and other large mammals do not take kindly to being surprised. Also take care when approaching a blind corner or rise.

At this altitude, and in the mountains, do take water with you, as well as a map and a small pack containing rain gear, sun screen and some food. Newcomers to the area should take it easy at first due to the altitude.

Skiing Lost Groomers Chute, Grand Targhee.
Photo: Grand Targhee Resort

SKIING & SNOWBOARDING

The central Rockies location of this area places it in prime skiing country. Due to a sparse local population, and restrictions on development, there are only three ski resorts. Despite this apparent lack of choice, there is in fact some of the finest skiing in the country to be found in this region.

Do be aware that these resorts lie more than 6,000ft above sea level and if you fly into the area, do take it easy on the first couple of days. This is particularly true at Jackson Hole Resort where the highest lift goes up to a heady 10,450ft.

If you have not skied or snowboarded before, you are advised to take lessons. These not only help prevent needless injuries from accidents caused by poor technique, they also will make your first few days more enjoyable as you will progress quicker. Some beginner snowboarders have mistakenly assumed that snowboarding is so easy to take up, that lessons are unnecessary. We have found that the opposite is the case. May be it has something to do with our age, somewhat higher than the average for the sport, but judging from what we have seen on the slopes, it does seem to be true for all ages. If you are a veteran skier, and perhaps looking for new challenges on the snow, try snowboarding. Once the prejudices are overcome, most find it a gas, and many refuse to return to skiing.

For the 1994 season, the three resorts banded together to offer the Jackson Hole Ski Three Multi Area Lift Voucher. Essentially a book of five vouchers, each voucher can be exchanged for a lift ticket at any of the resorts. This way you can experience all three easily.

1. Grand Targhee Ski Resort

Skiable Acres: 1,500   **Vertical drop:** 2,200ft
Base Elevation: 8,000ft   **Summit Elevation:** 10,200ft
Average yearly inches of snow: 500+ (42 ft!)
No. of runs: 46   **No. of lifts:** 4
10%Beginner   70%Intermediate   20%Advanced
Open: mid-November through mid-April

With an un-official motto of 'Snow from the heavens, not hoses', Grand Targhee is noted for its huge annual snowfall almost all of which is the best quality Rocky Mountain powder. Grand Targhee is a great 'small' resort, privately owned and managed by Mory and Carol Bergmeyer and is in our opinion, one of the best resorts for just cruising the trails and having a good time.

Lying in the shadow of the Tetons, some visitors to the Jackson Hole area may overlook this resort, perhaps under the impression that it has nothing to offer the extreme skier. While it is true that it is primarily an intermediate mountain, there are challenging powder runs and steep chutes and this year the Extreme Team Advanced Ski Clinics are being held at the Resort. The resort is also known for the off-piste snowcat skiing, and even Warren Miller films.

Serviced by only 4 lifts, but covering a huge 1,500 acres, the resort is a great place to avoid the crowds and seek out your own piece of skiable real estate. The layout has favored bowl-type skiing over piste, great for improving your turns. The north end of the resort is reputed to offer the best skiing. For those that hanker after heli-skiing, but can't justify the expense, there is always snowcat skiing. Snowcat skiing, where you are carried into otherwise inaccessible skiing terrain on the back of a snowcat vehicle, opens up a further 1,500 acres to the intermediate and expert skier. This is perhaps the best way to hit untracked powder snow after a new fall of snow.

The resort also offers a snow guarantee. If you are not happy with the snow conditions, hand in your full-day lift pass before 11.00am and receive a 'snow check' for another day.

The resort is located 42 miles from the town of Jackson, and there is a regular round trip bus service from Jackson and Teton Village (open December through to March).

Daily Ski Report: 1-800-TARGHEE.

Powder skiing at Grand Targhee.
Photo: Grand Targhee Resort

2. Jackson Hole Ski Resort

Skiable Acres: 2,500   **Vertical drop:** 4,139ft
Base Elevation: 6,311ft   **Summit Elevation:** 10,450ft
Average yearly inches of snow: 400
No. of runs: 46   **No. of lifts:** 10
10%Beginner   40%Intermediate   50%Advanced
Open: Early December through April

Jackson Hole Ski Resort is home to the largest vertical drop of any ski resort in the USA. Much of the resorts reputation stems from the extreme skiing available here - the infamous Corbett's Couloir is very exciting.

More recently however, the resort has been working to improve the facilities for the intermediate or beginner skier. Summer work crews have been out moderating some of the pistes for this reason, and although this has not pleased some of the locals and regulars who like the tough image, it should certainly please the recreational skier.

The main section of the Resort is Rendezvous Mountain that is covered with numerous black diamond runs and a few blues. The area off to the right of the resort - Apres Vous Mountain and Casper Bowl - is the domain of the intermediate with some slopes at the bottom aimed at the beginner.

Jewel in the Crown for the prospective extreme skier is the famous Corbett's Couloir which can best be described as intimidating. It is actually not too serious, as it has a pretty safe run-out. So if you totally blow it, you shouldn't come to too much harm. The Couloir is however subject to changing weather conditions, and the height of the jump in varies according to the depth of snow. Later in the season with greater snow depth, the jump may be quite short. There is usually a thick rope hanging down which can be used by the timid (sensible?) to bypass the jump.

Daily Ski Report: (307) 703-2291.

Skiing with a 'Western' flavor at Jackson Hole.
Photo: Bob Woodall & Jackson Hole Ski Resort

3. Snow King Ski Resort

Skiable Acres: 400	**Vertical drop:** 1,571ft
Base Elevation: 6,237ft	**Summit Elevation:** 7,808ft
Average yearly inches of snow: 250	
No. of runs: 17	**No. of lifts:** 4
15%Beginner 25%Intermediate	60%Advanced
Open: Late November through April	

Snow King Resort, known locally as Town Hill has under gone a major expansion of its downhill skiing capacity in time for the 1994/95 season. This includes a new 2,500ft Cougar Triple Chairlift and increased snow making and night skiing terrain.

A favorite with local skiers, Snow King is a 'small town' resort with a more intimate feel than the other two mega resorts. Situated on the edge of Jackson, it is one of the oldest resorts in the country dating from 1939.

Snow King may appear to be a pint-sized ski resort, but it has plenty to offer, without the big resort prices. There are the short steep narrow black diamond trails such as Belly Roll and Liftline to challenge the thrill seeker as well as good intermediate runs like Elk.

One of the resorts strengths is its proximity to the town center - within walking distance- allowing you to savor the unique flavor if Jackson nightlife. The Ski School is run by a veteran extreme skier, none other than Bill Briggs, the first man to ski down Grand Teton (not a trip currently offered by the School!).

The only ski resort in the region to offer night skiing, it is open until 9.30pm Tuesday through Saturday.

Snow King offers innovative pricing policies which allow you to tailor-make your skiing day. For instance, a two hour pass is $10, which is extendible in increments of one hour for a further $4 per hour. This is great for snagging a couple of powder hours before heading home, or going off on some other activity.

Daily Ski Report: (307) 733-5200.

Snow King Resort.

Photo: Snow King Resort

Nordic Centers

These centers offer groomed trails, set tracks and a backcountry skiing experience, all with nearby facilities. They are a great place to hone or learn new skills, especially skate skiing, and even try out new equipment. Some centers offer races and other competitive events. They tend to be less crowded than their alpine counterparts, and are certainly less expensive. They make a fine location for an afternoon workout.

Grand Targhee Nordic Center
10km of trails. A comprehensive nordic center with full facilities. Well-groomed trails, with both wooded and open areas. Also offers snowshoeing and dog sledding. For more information call 1-800-TARGHEE.

Jackson Hole Nordic Center
15km of trails. Full facilities, located at Teton Village. Quiet in contrast to its more famous next door neighbor. Both flat and undulating trails. For more information call (307) 739-2629.

Spring Creek Resort Nordic Center
20km of trails. Full facilities, located just west of Jackson. Double tracks. For more information call (307) 733-1004.

Teton Pines Cross-Country Ski Center
14km of trails. Full luxurious facilities including machine-groomed touring tracks and extra-wide skating tracks. Located 4 miles south of Teton Village on the Wilson Road. For more information call (307) 733-1005.

Togwotee Mountain Lodge Touring Center
20km of trails. Groomed tracks running through meadows, forests and slopes. A true mountain lodge experience with full facilities. Located at the bottom of Togwotee Pass, a one hour drive from Jackson. For more information call (307) 543-2847.

Skate skiing makes for a great workout. Grand Targhee Nordic Center.
Photo: Grand Targhee Resort

Backcountry Skiing & Snowboarding

The backcountry skier or snowboarder will find plenty to interest them in the Jackson Hole and Teton Valley area. Teton Pass has to be one of the premier locations for backcountry thrills in the USA, with its excellent road access and wide range of bowls and steep faces. We have distinguished here between cross-country skiing, a mix of flat, uphill and downhill skiing, and backcountry, where standard downhill gear (or for that matter, telemark) is carried up to a high point in anticipation of a fine run down. Similarly for snowboarding, although avoiding level ground is the most important criteria.

Accessing these areas can be difficult in certain conditions. Some areas are so popular that there will be a well-trodden trail. After a fresh fall of snow, or to less well-known sites, a pair of snowshoes would be very useful, especially for snowboarders.

Beware: Some of the more advanced descents are actually avalanche chutes! Call the 24hr Avalanche Information Line at (307) 733-2664 for current conditions before setting out, and exercise considerable care while out and about. Skinny Skis in Jackson and Backcountry Sports in Wilson are also good places to get local information. For safety's sake, always ski in groups, carry a shovel and avalanche transceiver per person, and know how to use them.

See the Cross-Country Skiing Section for more information on Teton Pass.

Photos above and opposite: Snowboarding on Mt. Glory.

Matt relates one of his improbable fishing tales.

SNOWMOBILING

During the winter months, one of the most practical ways of getting around this region, and indeed much of the high country in the West, is by snowmobile. The snowmobile opens up areas that can only otherwise be accessed by long, arduous skiing or snowshoeing trips. It is also a fun machine to ride, having an amazing ability to climb steep snow-covered slopes with aplomb, and cover great distances at speed.

There are many companies offering snowmobile tours or rentals in this area. If you have not ridden one before, it will only take a few minutes to run through the controls. They are pretty much automatic in operation, a simple squeeze of the throttle with your thumb will engage the automatic gearbox and off you go. To brake, you release the throttle, and the machine comes to a fairly prompt halt. For a faster stop, there is also a hand-operated brake. Most of the snowmobiles available for rent have a 440cc two-cycle engine which is capable of up to 65mph, conditions and regulations permitting.

On your first ride, the machine will probably feel rather twitchy, and this can be intimidating. After a while however, you will relax and find that the machine is really more steady and controllable that it at first appeared. Some trails may be rutted due to heavy snowmobile use. Under these circumstances, don't fight the ruts, just go with the flow. Then you can have fun!

The key to enjoying any sort of snowmobile trip is to wrap up warmly. As you can imagine, in sub-zero temperatures and at speeds of up to 45mph, it can be very cold, and for this reason most rental companies offer warm clothing, gloves and boots. Most modern machines should also have hand and foot warmers. You will also be required to wear a helmet, usually supplied, which should come equipped with a visor. Sunglasses will help to reduce glare from the snow, but note that skiing goggles may be uncomfortable under the helmet and are not recommended. Two person machines are also available but from our observations, being a passenger is a pretty miserable way to spend your time. The passenger, apart from getting a good view of the riders helmet, will also suffer from the cold and quite possibly terminal boredom. If you can at all afford it, a machine per person is far preferable.

One of the most popular trips is to ride into Yellowstone. In the Park, the only legal place to ride a snowmobile is on the highways. There is a maximum speed limit of 45mph, enforced by Rangers using radar speed traps. Just like motor vehicles, you are required to ride sensibly and obey traffic regulations. Tickets are issued for the usual traffic misdemeanours.

Yellowstone requires that all snowmobile operators have a valid motor vehicle operators license. Check on entrance to the Park for full requirements.

In Grand Teton National Park, certain roads are open to snowmobiles, check at the Visitor Centers. As with Yellowstone, off-road riding is prohibited, except on Jackson Lake which is open when the ice is safe.

Grand Teton National Park requires that you register for a permit for your snowmobile. These can be obtained at the Visitor Centers.

Tours are particularly useful if you are new to snowmobiling and want to get to know the sport with an experienced guide. In addition, if you want to see the sights in Yellowstone, and are not familiar with the Park, then you will probably get more out of your trip if you go with a tour group. On the other hand, if you have ridden before, and want the freedom to explore, then an unguided rental would be the best way to go.

Other locations for snowmobiling include Granite Creek, south of Jackson, Togwotee Pass to the east of Grand Teton National Park, the Gros Ventre area and the Teton Valley in Idaho.

A Day in Yellowstone On a Snowmobile

Probably the most popular guided snowmobile trip in the area is the run into Yellowstone. Known locally, and appropriately, as the 'Rocket Tour', the usual format is to visit Old Faithful, with wildlife viewing and geysers included.

The day starts early. We arrived at the Rocky Mountain Snowmobile Tours Office in Jackson at 7am, for a continental breakfast and collection of suit, helmet and boots. We were soon on our way to Flagg Ranch, a major port of call at the South end of the Park. Here, after a 1½hr drive, the snowmobiles are unloaded. A short lesson follows in the art of controlling the machines, as well as the importance of driving in single file, and within the speed limit. Greg, our guide, stressed the importance of keeping together so that he could monitor our progress at all times. We noticed another group had got spilt up, and as a result, some of the tour group ended up accidentally joining another tour, who had stopped for a break!

We then set off with a roar, and what was to become the familiar stink of two-cycle engines. Shortly after, we reached the Park South Entrance, where Greg paid our entrance fees before we set off into the Park.

The first ½ hour was a rather nerve-wracking experience. Recent heavy falls of snow had left the trail bumpy, and the regular passage of other machines had created ruts which seemed to catch our skids. At times it seemed as though the machine was in charge, rather than the other way around. In time however, we came to realize that it was in fact steadier than it appeared, and one could learn to relax and enjoy the ride.

Greg was sensitive to the fact that we were all novices, and made sure we had several stops along the way into Old Faithful, for both sight seeing and to relax.

We arrived at Old Faithful at around lunchtime, with about ½ an hour before the next expected eruption of Old Faithful. During this time Greg served us a tasty picnic lunch in the cosy warming hut nearby. There was even a nice touch of a table cloth to add color to otherwise fairly basic surroundings.

After watching Old Faithful, everyone piled back onto their machines and we headed out towards Biscuit Basin. Whenever we passed wildlife, Greg, who seemed to have an uncanny skill at animal spotting, would either pull-up for us to see, or just gesture in the direction as we went passed. When we did stop, he stressed the importance of keeping the snowmobile between us and the wildlife. The machine acts as a blind, and the disturbance to the animals is kept to a minimum.

Over the next couple of hours we visited each of the geyser basins going as far north as the Middle Geyser Basin. On this tour, time is limited. You do after all have to cover about 100 miles, so there is little time to linger. Occasionally we stopped to allow bison to cross the highway, they do after all have right of way. Strangely, despite the evident noise of the machines to us, the animals seemed not to care, and barely glanced in our direction.

Finally it was time to blast back to Flagg Ranch. We arrived back at 5pm, sore, but elated. The drive back to Jackson seemed to go faster than the outward trip, and we were soon relaxing tired muscles in our hotel's hot tub. What a day!

Snowmobiling in Yellowstone National Park

Snowshoeing on Jackson Lake.

S N O W S H O E I N G

In the last couple of years, snowshoeing has really taken off as a sport for just about anyone. Requiring little in the way of advanced techniques it is a sport that is within reach of all ages and levels of fitness. If you can hike, then you can snowshoe. modern snowshoes are considerably changed from the original models used by Yukon trappers. Hi-tech materials such as aluminum, rubber and neoprene make for lightweight and efficient designs. The ease with which it is possible to enter the backcountry in winter make this an excellent activity in this area.

All of the trails listed in the Hiking and Cross-Country Skiing sections could be done on snowshoes, although as snowshoeing is not as fast as skiing, you will need to bear in mind the shorter hours, and not try and tackle the longer trips. Do keep to one side of the ski tracks however.

Despite the ease with which you can get deep into the backcountry, it must still be stressed that the backcountry in winter is a potentially very hazardous place. Even with the best equipment, unless you have some basic skills such as the ability to map read, use a compass, read slopes for potential avalanche danger, and a good grasp of general mountain skills, it would be easy to get into serious trouble.

The best trails to start on in this area would be the relatively flat ones, such as Taggart Lake or Jenny Lake in the Tetons, or around the Upper Geyser Basin in Yellowstone National Park. Note that some areas of the Parks may be closed during the winter months to provide the wildlife with undisturbed areas. Check with the Rangers before setting out.

The best deal around has to be the Ranger-led snowshoe hikes in Grand Teton. These last about 2 hours and cover about 1½ miles. They start from the Moose Visitor Center and there is no charge. Snowshoes are also provided. What a deal! Reservations are required, call (307) 739-3399. The tours run from late-December through mid-March.

Snowshoe Design

Snow shoe design falls into several distinct categories, depending upon the original design, and the intended use of the shoe. All shoes have evolved from the very early designs that were the crude, but effective, shoes used by trappers in the mountains in the Rockies and Alaska.

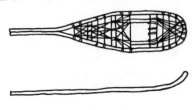

The Yukon

A traditional shape that is good for long, straightforward trails. The large area makes it good for coping with deep powder, and the slim shape allows the user to traverse hillsides easily. The long tail however makes this a difficult shoe to maneuver, and it is therefore not so good in thick woodland.

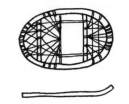

The Bearpaw

A compact shape makes the bearpaw a very maneuverable shoe. Its relatively small size makes it lighter on the feet. The almost round shape has the drawback of making it difficult to traverse hillsides however.

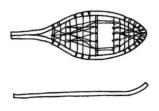

The Beaver Tail

A compromise between the Yukon and Bearpaw, the Beaver Tail is good for kicking steps uphill, but suffers from the rounded sides when traversing hillsides.

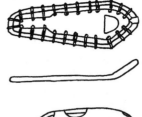

Western or Modern

a development from all three above shapes, the Western is the shoe from which most modern designs stem. Has a relatively small area, light in weight, and turned-up tail and toe.

Western Variant

The shoe shown here is one example of the most modern designs. Construction has evolved to aluminum frame and rubber deck.

Snowshoeing - how to have fun

One of the attractions of snowshoeing is the simplicity of the sport. Gear is kept to a minimum, and there are few real differences between models. There are however, a few subtleties that should be noted.

Size

Snowshoe size is determined by two factors. First the intended trails the shoer wants to traverse, and secondly, the weight of the user.

The snow on popular trails will tend, except after a recent snowstorm, to be well packed. For this reason, smaller, lighter, shoes will suffice. In these conditions, with a light pair of snowshoes, jogging will even be possible. For off-trail use, or after a recent heavy fall of snow, the smaller snowshoes will sink into the snow making the going very tiring. The same will be true if you are carrying a heavy pack. Under these conditions, a larger snowshoe will be required.

Your weight will also be important in picking a snowshoe large enough to support your weight without breaking through the snow crust, while being as small as possible to reduce weight.

A good tip is to rent before you buy.

Bindings

Traditionally, the bindings on snowshoes were a simple lace system which attached the snowshoe to your boots. This system had the advantage of being simple, robust and easy to repair in the field. These are still important attributes, particularly if you are going deep into the backcountry and need to be able to depend on your equipment.

More modern bindings may be more comfortable and easier to put on. These include such methods as neoprene sleeves into which lightweight boots or even sneakers fit. These sorts of bindings are more suitable for urban or well travelled trails where help is never far away, and the snow well-packed on the trails.

Ski Poles

Ski poles are very important. They help with stability when on the move, and should you fall over, they make getting up considerably easier. If you are attracted to snowshoeing for fitness reasons, they will give you an upper body workout as well, just like cross-country skiing.

Canoeing on Jenny Lake.

Photo: R. DuMais

Grading of Rivers

Class I	Easy	Fast water with few or no obstacles.
Class II	Novice	Simple rapids with some rocks or snags.
Class III	Intermediate	More technical rapids, serious snags. Technical skill required.
Class IV	Advanced	Powerful water with many hazards.
Class V	Expert	Violent water.
Class VI	Extreme	Right at the limits of the sport.

Note: Grading of rivers is subjective at best, and should only be used as a rough guide. Always check locally before setting out, and bear in mind that conditions can change quickly.

WATERSPORTS

This region offers several very large lakes, as well as a range of rivers with both mellow and whitewater stretches. It is not unreasonable to suggest there is something for everyone. Many of the waters have wonderful scenery, and opportunities for seeing wildlife.

If you don't have your own boat, there are plenty of places that will rent you anything from a kayak right up to large river rafts.

Due to the snow melt, the rivers will have heavy flows during the Spring and into early Summer. While this does make for interesting whitewater, it should be noted that the water will be very cold, and a wetsuit may be a good idea. Also, the water is unfit for drinking, so keep your mouth shut if you fall in!

River running is potentially a serious proposition, as it can be very easy to set off, but difficult to avoid problems if the water flow is high and fast. Care should be exercised before setting out, and while a stretch of river may be nominally graded as Class II, for instance, unusually high (or low) water could make it considerably harder. It is always a good idea to check locally as to the state of the river, and to inspect on foot any section that cannot be seen clearly from water level.

In the National Parks, all boats need to be registered for a permit, for which a small fee is charged. Check with the Visitor Centers. In addition, a wide range of regulations cover the use of boats in the area, including the requirement that each person has access to their own U.S. Coast Guard-approved personal flotation device. You are strongly advised to check for local information before setting out on the rivers or lakes, as conditions change, as do the regulations. Contact Yellowstone Park Information at (307) 344-7381, Grand Teton Park Information at (307) 739-3300.

Lakes

All these lakes are deep and cold, and due to their size, can become dangerous places in bad weather.

Yellowstone National Park

Yellowstone Lake

Yellowstone Lake is open to both sail and motor vessels, although the southern arms of the lake are regulated with a 5 mph speed limit. The extreme ends of South Arm and South-East Arm are restricted to hand-propelled craft only. The main access points are the boat ramps at Grant and the marina at Bridge Bay.

Lewis Lake

Access to Lewis Lake is via the boat ramp at Lewis Lake Campground. Motorized vessels must stay on the lake, while hand-propelled craft may venture up the Lewis River to access Shoshone Lake. This short, 3 mile, stretch of river is basically flat and shallow.

Shoshone Lake

Shoshone Lake is only open to hand-propelled vessels. There are a number of back country campsites accessible from the lake shore that make a good destination for a overnight canoe trip. Do remember to book one before setting out.

Grand Teton National Park

Jackson Lake

Jackson Lake is open to motor and sailing vessels up to 40ft in length. Water skiing is also allowed. Sailboats, windsurfers and jet skis are only allowed on Jackson Lake. The only access points for boats transported by vehicles are at Leek's Marina, Colter Bay boat ramp, Signal Mountain boat ramp and Spalding Bay boat ramp.

Jenny Lake

There is a restriction of 7.5 horse power for motorized vessels on Jenny Lake. The only access point for boats transported by vehicle is at the Jenny Lake boat ramp which is reached from the Lupine Meadows Trailhead road at the south end of the lake. Jenny Lake also has a commercial ferry boat operation which runs to and from the Hidden Falls dock on the west side of the lake.

Other lakes

The following lakes are open to hand-propelled craft only: Phelps, Emma Matilda, Two Ocean, Taggart, Bradley, Bearpaw, Leigh and Sting Lakes.

All other lakes in the park are closed to boating.

Other Areas

Lower Slide Lake near Kelly is open to boating and canoeing as well as being popular with windsurfers.

Rivers

Yellowstone National Park

Lewis River

The only section of river open to boating is the Lewis River, also known as the Lewis-Shoshone Channel which is navigable only by hand-propelled craft. Depending on the water depth, portage may be necessary as it is shallow in places.

Grand Teton National Park

Snake River

The Snake River has two sections running through this area, a northern piece that flows into Jackson Lake from the John D. Rockefeller, Jr., Memorial Parkway, and a southern section that leaves the east side of Jackson Lake and flows south.

The northern section is the least floated, and offers a more wilderness experience. There are two sections;

a: Southgate Launch to Flagg Ranch

Flowing down through Flagg Canyon, this section is rated Class III, and is not recommended for open canoes. In the Spring this section can involve big water and should only be attempted by advanced paddlers. In lower water flows it can be even harder. Launch at a point ½ mile south of the South Entrance to Yellowstone.

b: Flagg Ranch to Lizard Creek

A fine section for wildlife viewing, it is rated at about Class II and the braiding of the river, and occasional log jams make for an interesting run. It is about a 10 mile run.

The southern section can be seen as having four separate sections, ranging in difficulty from easy to advanced.

c: Jackson Lake Dam to Pacific Creek Landing

This is the easiest section of the Snake River, and is the only one recommended for beginners. Flowing through the scenic Oxbow Bend area, there are ample opportunities for spotting wildlife. Moose are often seen around here. About 2½ miles in length.

d: Pacific Creek Landing to Deadmans Bar

The river becomes more difficult in this section. It is rated at Class II and is basically fairly straightforward with riffles and shallows. There is an Eagle Closure section where foot travel is prohibited within a ½ mile up and down-stream, signs are placed to indicate this. A 10½ mile section.

e: Deadmans Bar to Moose

Not a good section for inexperienced boaters. Even experienced boaters are recommended to go with someone who has local knowledge of the river on their first trip down. Rated Class II for technical difficulty, the complex braiding and numerous log jams make it a serious outing. One area, called The Maze, is particularly unpleasant and should be avoided at all costs. Stay on the main channel which has the greatest water volume, wherever possible. There is also an Eagle Closure section in the lower half. 10 miles in length.

f: Moose to Wilson Bridge

Mostly easy, this is rated at Class II with some braiding and, depending on water level and snags, there may be several tricky sections. 15 miles in length.

g: Wilson Bridge to South Park Bridge (Highway 89)

Class II, with much braiding. As it travels through private property, shore landings should be avoided. 13 miles, with a possible takeout off the Fall Creek Road at the 8 mile point.

h: South Park Bridge (Highway 89) to West Table River Access

After the South Park Bridge, the river narrows and flows through a small canyon. This section is Class II, and is a fine scenic stretch. There are several takeouts along here, starting at Astoria Hot Springs, followed by Pritchard Landing and Elbow Campground.

i: West Table River Access to Sheep Gulch

The most popular section for whitewater rafters, this is an exciting stretch with some fun big water, including the famous Big Kahuna, Lunch Counter and Rope Rapids. Depending on the level of the water, it can be Class III through to Class V. If you are unfamiliar with this section, you should check locally at one of the sports stores, such as Rent-A-Raft at Hoback Junction, as to the current conditions. Due to its popularity it can be crowded from early morning through mid-afternoon.

Gros Ventre River

There are two sections of the Gros Ventre River that offer interesting river running. The upper section from Bridge Creek down to Warden Bridge Landing is Class I. The middle section from Warden Bridge down through Upper Slide Lake and on to Lower Slide Lake and the takeout at Atherton Campground, is Class III. The lower section from the outlet of Lower Slide Lake, reached by a dirt road off the highway which takes you down to the outlet bridge, is 3 miles in length and Class III/IV. The takeout is at the National Park Boundary where the river comes close to the pavement of the highway.

Hoback River

The Hoback River takes the picturesque Hoback Canyon down to Hoback Junction. The main section, from the confluence of Granite Creek on to Hoback Junction is Class II/III. Keep an eye out for wildlife, particularly near the Stinking Springs.

Granite Creek

During the early part of the summer there can be enough water in Granite Creek to make it an interesting river. Check locally for more information.

Buffalo Fork of the Snake River

Flowing down to join the Snake River at Moran Junction, the Buffalo Fork has a stretch of Class II water which can be of interest. Put-in at Turpin Meadows Campground. The takeout is at Moran Junction. There is also a take-out off the Buffalo Valley Road about a mile from Highway 287. 13 miles in length.

Boating on Lewis Lake.

Radio-tagging porcupines, part of a on-going research project.
Photo: Great Plains Wildlife Institute

WILDLIFE VIEWING

Yellowstone National Park needs little in the way of introduction as a major wildlife viewing location. The large mammals that live in the Park are world famous, almost celebrities, and for many are the crown jewels of the Park Service. They also often feature in news items around the world for reasons ranging from wolf re-introduction, bison shootings, to bear attacks. Grand Teton is also known for its wildlife, although they are possibly not as easy to see.

Sadly, for some, the message that is constantly relayed to visitors to the Parks, that of not approaching the wildlife too close, is still not getting through. Every year brings a new spate of maulings of tourists who do not understand that wild animals are exactly that. Wild. We implore anyone who wants to view wildlife to do it in such a way as to not disturb the animals. A good rule of thumb is that if the animal you are viewing changes its behavior due to your actions, then you have disturbed it. On a recent trip down after climbing on Grand Teton, Freddie and Matt came across a black bear and her cub. They were rewarded with a good view of the two, before the bears wandered off into the woods. As they carried on down the trail, they encountered several groups of people wandering through the undergrowth searching for the bears. Evidently the word that bears were around had spread like wildfire. These people were in effect chasing the bears. There is a fine distinction between wildlife viewing, and harassment.

In this chapter we will suggest some suitable places to go and view wildlife, in particular the large mammals, and also look at various government and private wildlife institutes and centers. The best source of information as to where to see the wildlife is often the Rangers at the Visitors Centers. They have the most up-to-date knowledge, and will be happy to advise you where to go viewing. As with bird watching, the most profitable times of day are first thing in the morning, and at dusk.

Wildlife Viewing Locations

Yellowstone National Park

Lamar Valley
Bison, elk and pronghorn antelope may be seen in the valley.

Hayden Valley
Bison are very common in the Hayden Valley, and often cause minor traffic jams as they wandered back and forth across the highway. It is possible to get very close up views, perhaps even too close, from inside your car along here. Moose may be seen in the evenings, and sometimes grizzlies can be seen in the meadows on the east shore of the Yellowstone River. Waterfowl, including the venerable white pelican and trumpeter swan.

Fishing Bridge and Pelican Creek
A major grizzly habitat, you may be lucky to see them in this area. Moose may be seen in the creek in the evening, and waterfowl fish the waters of the creek and Yellowstone Lake.

Antelope Creek
A popular early-evening viewing point is from the pull-ins on the Tower-Canyon highway overlooking Antelope Creek. This is prime grizzly habitat and also home to elk. This area is closed to human off-road travel to give the bears refuge from human intrusion. View only from the highway.

Mt. Washburn
Probably the only place in the park where visitors commonly see big horn sheep. The sheep inhabit the rocky slopes during the summer months and are easily photographed. Watch for yellow-bellied marmots in the rocks near the summit.

Midway and Upper Geyser Basins
Elk and bison may be seen around the geyser basins.

Mammoth
During the rut in the Fall, elk start moving into the town of Mammoth for the winter. This is an excellent opportunity to see them, and hear the elk bugling.

Elk feeding on the alfalfa pellets in the National Elk Refuge, Jackson Hole.

Grand Teton National Park

Willow Flats

This fresh water marsh area is excellent habitat for a variety of waterfowl, beaver and moose.

Oxbow Bend

A meandering section of the Snake River, one of its most common visitors is the white pelican who may be joined by osprey and eagle all fishing in the Snake. Beavers are usually only active at night, but you may be lucky to see them early in the morning or late evening. Moose are also often seen in the area, as are on occasion, elk.

Blacktail Ponds

Abandoned beaver ponds have produced a grass meadow, a favorite spot for moose. Elk may also be seen in the evening.

Snake River

A variety of birds of prey live on or near the river. Bison and elk often graze in the sagebrush flats near the river, and moose inhabit the shores.

Timbered Island

An 'island' of forest surrounded by sagebrush, this area provides shelter in the heat of the day for a variety of animals such as antelope, deer and elk.

Lower Slide Lake

Eagles and waterfowl are commonly seen around the lake and look out for hawks as well. Big horn sheep live on the rocky outcrops above the lake, and bear may be seen in the valley.

Stinking Springs

Hot subterranean water bubbling up into the Hoback River emits a strong sulphur odor that gives this area its name. In the area, mule deer and big horn sheep can be seen, and in winter elk live on the slopes. In the spring elk calves are born in the area. The occasional coyote may also be spotted around here.

Opposite top: Specially designed viewing vans used for wildlife viewing. Photo: Great Plains Wildlife Institute.

Organized Wildlife Tours and Centers

National Elk Refuge

During the 1800's there were an estimated 25,000 elk in Jackson Hole. As more people moved into the valley, more of the traditional wintering grounds of the elk were encroached upon. The Elk Refuge was created in 1912 in response to concern over the survival of the herds. Originally some 2,700 acres, it now covers an area of 24,000 acres. It is now estimated that 15,000 elk winter in Jackson Hole, and 50% within the Refuge boundaries. The elk move into the Refuge in late October, and leave for higher ground at the end of April. The young are usually born during early June. During the harshest part of the winter when there is not sufficient food for the elk, additional food in the form of alfalfa hay pellets is provided. For the visitor, the Refuge is a winter attraction. Open 10.00am to 4.00pm from late-December to late-March, tours go in amongst the herds. This is a unique experience, and not to be missed. Tours are on a horse-drawn sleigh and last about 45 minutes. Wrap up warmly!

For information, contact the The Refuge Manager, National Elk Refuge, Box C, Jackson, WY 83001. (307) 733-9212. Tours start from the National Wildlife Art Museum, located just north of Jackson on the highway towards Grand Teton National Park. The Art Museum itself is also worth a visit in its own right.

Jackson National Fish Hatchery

Operated by the United States Fish and Wildlife Service. The main aim of the hatchery is to produce eggs, and raise fish for the stocking of waters in the region. Primarily a service for National Parks, they also provide fish for State Parks. Of a lesser priority is the provision of fish to private waters that are open to public fishing. The Hatchery raises some 1,000,000 Snake River cutthroat trout and Lake Trout (Mackinaw) annually. Action begins in the Fall as the trout begin to spawn.

Located on National Elk Refuge land, 4 miles north of Jackson. For more information, write to Jackson National Fish Hatchery, 1500 Fish Hatchery Road, Jackson, WY 83001.

Teton Science School

An independently owned, non-profit center offering natural science programs for all ages. Residential and non-residential courses are offered, ranging from $50 to over $2,000. Subjects covered range from Animal Tracks & Signs, The Night Sky, to Entomology for Fishermen. Open year round, the school offers adventures in science for all ages.

The School is located in the south-east section of Grand Teton National Park, 3½ miles north-west of Kelly. For more information, write to PO Box 68, Kelly, WY 83011. Tel: (307) 733-4765.

Wildlife Safaris

Organized by the Great Plains Wildlife Institute, a private company that operates under Federal permits in the region. The Institute offers a range of tours from short half-day wildlife safaris, to full day safaris incorporating scientific research, and on up to six day expeditions. They use specially designed vans with viewing hatches, binoculars and viewing scopes.

The half-day tours, called Sunrise & Sunset Expeditions, last about 4 hours. You travel in the company of a staff naturalist and learn about the animals in their habitats, as well as viewing them. Animals most likely seen on a safari would include bison, moose, elk, bighorn sheep, coyote, bald eagles and trumpeter swans.

The Full-Day Expedition, in the company of a wildlife biologist, is a more in-depth experience. After a morning spent viewing, you will then participate in actual research projects such as tracking radio-collared animals.

The Six-Day Expeditions involve a variety of excursions and research projects. Touring throughout the region, accommodation is of a very high level, and you will take an in-depth look into the wildlife of the area.

For more information, contact the Institute at PO Box 7580, Jackson Hole, Wyoming, 83001. Tel: (307) 733-2623.

Targhee Institute

A non-profit organization created to increase educational and cultural opportunities in the Greater Yellowstone area. Located at Grand Targhee Ski and Summer Resort on the west side of the Tetons, just east of Driggs, Idaho.

Offering multi-day courses for younger people in subjects such as Nature Through a Camera Lens, the Big Ones: Lions, Bears and Wolves, and Rock and Roll Geology. For older folk there are courses in the Eiderhostel Program in subjects such as Teton Natural History and Liquid Gold:Water in the American West.

For more information contact the Institute at PO Box 335, Alta, WY 83422. Tel: (307) 353-8566.

Yellowstone Institute

The Yellowstone Institute, operating on behalf of the Yellowstone National Park, offers an alternative to the typical "through-the-windshield" visitor experience. With more than 80 courses, one to five days in length, in natural and cultural history, it is well placed in the Lamar Valley for nature study.

For more information, contact the Institute at Box 117, Yellowstone National Park, WY 82190. Tel: (307) 344-2294.

The Authors on the summit of Grand Teton, July 1994.
Freddie on the left, Matt on the right.

Photo: R. DuMais

A F T E R W O R D

A s we finish writing in early 1995, we can look back on a fascinating year spent largely in Wyoming working on this book. An enduring impression we both took away with us was not only the grandeur of the region, but also the friendliness of the locals and evident love they have for their own backyard. While National Parks seem to be popping up all over the country, these two are amongst the finest in the country, and long may they stay that way.

We were also struck by the helpfulness of the Park Rangers, and their evident love for their work, and the Parks. We can only marvel at their patience when being asked questions like "When do the Elk turn into Moose?", without groaning or toppling over.

Like many, we were heartened by the re-introduction of wolves in 1995, and hope that it is successful. The threats to these Parks are many and varied, and all positive steps to keep it a naturally-sustaining wilderness, as much as possible, should be taken.

About the Authors

The authors are Englishmen who have made Boulder, Colorado, their home.

Matt Harding

A mountaineer at heart, Matt came to the USA after falling in love with Colorado during a skiing vacation in 1991. He now runs a publishing company in Boulder, Colorado and still finds time to climb and travel. Matt shares many of his adventures with his wife, Babette.

Freddie Snalam

Freddie arrived in Boulder, Colorado having sailed the Atlantic in 1980 on his quest for sunshine and adventure. Although worldwide travels are being planned on a regular basis, some local commitments keep him on a even keel. These include graphic art, music and his most prestigious job - owner and proprietor of the World Famous Freddie's Hot Dog Cart on the Pearl Street Mall in Boulder.

Reference 1
Outfitters & Schools

Note: This is only a very small selection of the companies operating in this large area.

BALLOON FLIGHTS
Rainbow Balloon Flights, Box 20066, Jackson, WY 83001 Tel: (307) 733-0470
Wyoming Balloon Company, Box 2578, Jackson, WY 83001 Tel: (307) 739-0900

CROSS-COUNTRY SKIING
Rendezvous Ski Tours, 219 Highland Way, Victor, ID 83455 Tel: (208) 787-2906

DOG SLEDDING
Jackson Hole Iditarod Sled Dog Tours, Box 1940, Jackson, WY 83001
Tel: (307) 733-7388

FISHING GUIDES
Fort Jackson River Trips, Box 1176, Jackson, WY 83001 Tel: (307) 733-2583
Jack Dennis Sportsmans Travel Service, PO Box 3369, Jackson, WY 83001
Tel: (307) 733-3270
John Henry Lee Outfitters Inc., Box 8368, Jackson, WY 83001 Tel: (307) 733-9441
UP Stream Anglers, Box 30106, Jackson, WY 83001 Tel: (307) 733-8057
Westbank Anglers, Box 523, 3670 N.Moose-Wilson Road, Teton Village, WY 83025 Tel: (307) 733-6483

FLOAT TRIPS
Barker-Ewing Float Trips, Box 100, Moose, WY 83012 Tel: (307) 733-1800
Barker-Ewing River Trips, Box 3032, 45 W. Broadway, Jackson, WY 83001
Tel: (307) 733-1000
Mad River Boat Trips, Inc., Box 2222, 1060 S. Hwy. 89, Jackson, WY 83001
Tel: (307) 733-6203

FLYING & GLIDING
Grand Valley Aviation, Driggs, Idaho Tel: (208) 354-8131
Jackson Hole Aviation, Box 3829, Jackson, WY 83001. Tel: (307) 733-4767

HORSEBACK RIDING
A-OK Corral, Box 3878, Jackson, WY 83001 Tel: (307) 733-6556
GTLC Jackson Lake Lodge Corral, Box 250, Moran, WY 83013 Tel : (307) 543-2811

Togwotee Mountain Lodge, Box 91, Moran, WY 83013 Tel: (307) 543-2847

HUNTING
All American Outfitters, Box 745, Wilson, WY 83014 Tel: (307) 733-9434
Bridger-Teton Outfitters, Star Route Box 347, Jackson, WY 83001
Tel: (307) 733-7745
Bud Nelson Big Game Outfitters & Guides,Box 409, Jackson, WY 83001
Tel: (307) 733-2843
Jackson Hole Wilderness Adventures, Box 8264, Jackson, WY 83001
Tel: (307) 733-2468

MOUNTAINEERING AND ROCK CLIMBING
Exum Mountain Guides, Box 56, Moose, WY 83012 Tel: (307) 733-2297
Jackson Hole Mountain Guides, Box 7477, 165 N. Glenwood, Jackson, WY
83001 Tel: (307) 733-4979

PARAGLIDING
Jackson Hole Paragliding, Box 8287, Jackson, WY 83001 Tel:(307) 739-8620

SNOWMOBILING
Flagg Ranch Village, PO Box 187, Moran, WY 83013 Tel: (307) 543-2356
Fort Jackson Snowmobile Tours, Box 631, Jackson, WY 83001 Tel: (307) 733-6850
Rocky Mountain Snowmobile Tours, Box 820, 1050 S. Hwy. 89, Jackson, WY
83001 Tel: (307) 733-2237 & 1-800-647-2561
Togwotee Mountain Lodge, Box 91, Moran, WY 83013 Tel: (307) 733-8800

WATERSPORTS
Snake River Kayak School, Box 3482, Jackson, WY 83001 Tel: (307) 733-2623
Rent-A-Craft, HC 66 15-S, Jackson, WY 83001 Tel: (307) 733-2728

WILDLIFE EXPEDITIONS
Great Plains Wildlife Institute, PO Box 7580, Jackson, WY 83001
Tel: (307) 733-2623

Reference 2
Further Reading

General Interest

A Field Guide to Yellowstone's Geysers, Hot Springs and Fumeroles -
Carl Schreier

Bear Attacks - Stephen Herrero

Guardians of Yellowstone - Dan R. Sholly with Steven M. Newman

Nature Guide to Jackson Hole - Olaus J. Murie

Track of the Grizzly - Frank C. Craighead, Jr., Ph.D.

Maps

Grand Teton National Park - Trails Illustrated

Hiking Map & Guide to Grand Teton National Park - Earthwalk Press

Mountain Biking in the Jackson Hole Area - Bikecentennial

Yellowstone National Park - Trail Illustrated

Avalanches

The Avalanche Book - Betsy R. Armstrong & Knox Williams

Birding

Birds of Grand Teton National Park and the Surrounding Area - Bert Raynes

Cross-Country Skiing

50 Ski Tours in Jackson Hole & Yellowstone - Richard DuMais

Fishing

The Wyoming Angling Guide - Fothergill & Sterling

Yellowstone Fishing Guide - Robert E. Charlton

Geology

Roadside Geology - William J. Fritz

Hiking

50 Jackson Hole Hiking Trails - Rebecca Woods

Day Hiking Yellowstone - Tom Carter

Yellowstone Trails - Mark C. Marschall

Mountain Biking

Mountain Biking Guide to Jackson Hole - Keith & Diane Beuefiel

Mountaineering & Rock Climbing

Jackson Hole, A Sport Climbing and Bouldering Guide - Joe Sottile

Climber's Guide to the Teton Range - Leigh Ortenburger

Selected Climbs in the Teton Range - Jim Olson

Teton Classics - Richard Rossiter

Watersports

Paddle and Portage - Dan Lewis

INDEX

Useful Telephone Numbers
In an emergency, Dial 911

National Parks & Forests
Grand Teton National Park Headquarters: (307) 739-3600
Yellowstone National Park Headquarters: (307) 344-7381
Shoshone National Forest: (307) 527-6241
Bridger-Teton National Forest: (307) 739-5500
Targhee National Forest: (208) 624-3151

Chambers of Commerce
Billings, MT: (406) 245-4111
Cody, WY: (307) 587-2297
Gardiner, MT: (406) 848-7971
Livingston, MT: (406) 222-0850
West Yellowstone, MT: (406) 646-7701
Bozeman, MT: (406) 586-5421
Red Lodge, MT: (446-1718
Cooke City, MT: (406) 838-2265
Jackson, WY: (307) 733-3316
Dubois, WY: (307) 455-2556
East Yellowstone, WY: (307) 587-9595

Game and Fish
Wyoming Game and Fish: 1-800-423-4113
Stop Poaching: 1-800-442-4331

Miscellaneous
American Avalanche Institute: (307) 733-3315
Avalanche and Weather 24hr Information Line: (307) 733-2664

Also by the same Authors:

Get Out Of Town! A Comprehensive Guide to Outdoor
Activities in the Boulder,Colorado area.
ISBN: 1-884294-00-6   Price: $14.95

Further copies of this book and the above book can be ordered
from your local book store, or ordered direct from the publisher.

Shipping & Handling Charges $2.00 per book

All Points Publishing, Inc
PO Box 4832,
Boulder,
CO. 80306
USA